Daughter of the King

Daughter of the King

WAIT, WHERE'S MY CROWN?!

Kaylin Koslosky and Megan Finegan

ISBN: 1534720340
ISBN 13: 9781534720343

Cover artwork by Andrea Cott.
Cover layout and website design by J. Patrick Finegan.
Copy editing by Jane Cavolina.

This book is dedicated to Mama Mary—who embodies true femininity and radiates the beauty and selfless love that we wish to capture in this book, and in our own lives.
Thank you for all of your guidance and love.
This book is for you.

Contents

Two Things You Should Know Before You Begin

1. For the majority of this book we will be writing together with one line of thought—which explains why you will be reading the word "we" a lot. This works out well for us because we have practically been completing each other's sentences since the third grade. However, at times we will split to share more personal stories about some topics. When we do, we will identify ourselves as either Megan or Kaylin so that you can begin to piece together our different stories— also so that we don't confuse the heck out of you.

2. We use a lot of research studies and quotes throughout this book, so you will be seeing little superscripted numbers at the end of those lines in order to reference the source. For example, the number "3" would denote that we used source #3 in the bibliography for that quote or study reference.

Enjoy!

Introduction

ALL RIGHT, WE KNOW YOU just settled into reading this book, and if you're like us you probably don't want to move, but humor us real quick. Get up, bring the book, and go stand in front of a mirror. What do you see? Really look at yourself. What things stand out to you?

We'll wait . . .

How many flaws did you count? We just did it, and we each counted at least five right away, as if we already knew them without looking. And we aren't alone. One study showed that women experience about thirteen negative thoughts about their body daily, and 97 percent of women admit to hating their body at least once each day.[14] Did you think of even one positive thing? We didn't on our first try. So now go back and take another look. *Really* look this time. If any negative thoughts come up, push them away and think of at least three positive things you love about your body.

It's not as easy, huh?

This is the primary reason we chose to write this book. There is a fundamental problem in the way that women are being viewed, both by themselves and others, and how they are being treated as a result. By the time we got to college this distortion was even more painfully obvious than it had been in high school. The social norm of college nowadays seems to magnify our "problems" and point out how far from "perfect" we really are. It makes it hard to find yourself when you are being told who you should be. As we worked through this common struggle—seeking to fit in, to be beautiful, to be successful, to be liked—we realized just how consuming this can be. Our hidden desire to discover who we are, the purpose of our lives, and what true beauty means, continued to fight against the people we found ourselves becoming.

It is difficult to remain true to yourself when you aren't even sure who you are yet. Staying true to your values, morals, and faith when the world may be loudly disagreeing with you is hard, and it often seems much more fun to live in the moment, without considering the consequences. Let's face it: it would definitely be easier to do whatever you want whenever you want to! But would it really be fulfilling? Is that really what we are all searching for?

As we realized how hard the battle is between the conflicting desires within us, we sought the advice of others, we read books, and we better learned the teachings of the Church and the Bible. We learned that in all of this great wisdom there was one thing missing—the perspective of a young woman: Someone who is living the battle, suffering persecution from the media, and living with the expectation that she will look like a model, be sweet but sexy, tough but gentle, laid back but always put-together, skinny but curvy. We needed someone who knows what it is like to grow up with the pressures of these contradictions and impossible expectations. Someone who is not looking at our generation and wishing better for it, but is living within it—experiencing all this here and now, *today*. Once the two of us began talking about it, we recognized that we are both passionate about this topic, and that we have learned parallel lessons despite our drastically different stories.

We have been best friends since third grade. We've grown up together and watched as we each took very different paths from girl to woman. Between the two of us, we have seen or experienced almost everything that the world offers to women in high school and college. We hope that you may be able to see a piece of your story reflected in our own journeys, failures, and realizations, and find a new perspective on it. We hope that by the end of the book you will have come to a greater understanding of the unique beauty within you and of the greater life for which you have been created. We will also provide you with tools and exercises that will help you to incorporate these new understandings realistically into your life.

So without further ado, let the journey begin!

PART I

We Choose What the Mirror Reflects

1. "The Perfect Woman"

Good news, ladies! We have found what you need to be the perfect woman. This recipe will make every man fall in love with you, because men themselves created their picture-perfect lady in a *Men's Health* magazine survey. It's *so* realistic . . . ! Ready? Here's what you need to have: brown hair, small feet, large breasts, narrow hips, a permanent smile, long legs, intelligence, lots of red clothing or lipstick, and the astounding ability to laugh at every single one of a man's jokes.[7] Oh . . . is that all? Because it makes perfect sense that if you have huge boobs you'll have tiny hips. And with those amazon long legs, you'll naturally have cute, little feet for your man to massage. And of course everyone should be a brunette, since brown hair means you're smarter and will be more successful. Also, we all just got back from the tropics, so we're perfectly tan at all times, too, right? Ha!

This is probably one of the most ridiculous things we've ever seen, but it was the first story that popped up when we Googled what the perfect woman should look like—the first that wasn't a link to a porn site (which is a whole other issue that we will discuss later). What a terrifying sight this woman would be in real life. These things don't go together—it's just not natural! Yet these are the kind of lies that we grow up seeing and hearing. Normally the media is a bit sneakier about it, though, thanks to the invention of Photoshop, which allows magazines (and other media) to create an impossible level of perfection, which women then desire to embody and men desire to love. Can you see anything wrong with this picture?

Imagine being that woman on the cover of a magazine. Everyone sees you as a perfect picture of beauty to be coveted, but you can hardly even recognize yourself. Your neck has been lengthened, your breasts enlarged, your eyes reshaped, your skin enhanced, your lips plumped, your hair amplified—you get the point. Nobody looks like that. It's not *real* and it is definitely not *true beauty*. We are bombarded with such fake images on a daily basis, constantly reminding us that we simply aren't good enough even if we are the models on the cover of the magazine.

With messages like this in our heads, it makes sense that four out of five women in the United States are unhappy with their appearance.[14] It would be all too easy to blame this problem on the media, the models, and Photoshopping, since they are what creates and popularizes these false images of beauty. But the problem is, *we can't control the media*! Sure, we should work to change it and not support women being distorted in this way, but that doesn't help us deal with that pressure right now.

So what do we do? Is our search for beauty hopeless? Is there nothing we can do but wait for the media to alter its portrayal of women, and in doing so alter the opinions we have of ourselves? No. No amount of media revolution, as great as that would be, will change the fact that "You are not pretty enough" is already ingrained in our minds.

What we need to do is focus on what we *can* control. We can control how much power we give these false images and how much we listen to the judgments of others. We can control what we say to ourselves when we look in the mirror and what we say about other girls walking by. We *choose* which lies we believe about beauty. A woman is the crown of creation—the most beautiful creation on Earth. Our beauty is intended to reveal the beauty of heaven, the beauty of something beyond this world, and the beauty and mystery of our Creator. How often have you heard your beauty described like that? Not often enough, that's for sure. This is the way that we need to come to perceive beauty.

However, moving away from believing (whether we choose to admit it or not) that beauty is what we see in those Photoshopped images, to believing that beauty is deeper and capable of existing in all women, not just one type of woman, is a tough journey. Like any journey, it is going to take commitment, but we promise you it is worth it. Nothing will positively influence every aspect of your life more than coming to truly believe that you are beautiful exactly the way you are, that you are immensely loved by the One who created you, and that your beauty is a gift given to better the world and lead those in this world to seek something greater—something deeper.

Let's embark on this journey together.

2. WOMEN AS SEX OBJECTS

The main problem we encounter on this journey is discovering the purpose of beauty in the first place. The beauty of women has become distorted to the point that it no longer calls others to long for the deeper beauty of heaven and of the Creator. We are not the creator of our own beauty; we are a gift to the world as a reminder of the beauty that we were all made for. However, we are being taught that *we* are the end goal and that our bodies are ours to use to attract others to ourselves. We are told that our ability to be loved relies on our ability to have a beautiful body. That's a lot of pressure, being the *creator of your own beauty.*

We grow up with the idea that we should use our bodies to get and keep a guy's attention. All the while we are unknowingly teaching ourselves to base more and more of our self-worth on whether or not we are able to "turn heads." We keep those false images of beauty filed away in our minds, ready to compare ourselves to them at any given time. In an attempt to fill our deep desire to be loved and seen as beautiful, many of us fall captive to this lie that beauty is something that must be obtained rather than something from within.

The moment we look at ourselves in a mirror and only see our bodies, we are objectifying ourselves. We are separating our bodies from our souls and our hearts. It is one of the most dangerous things we can do. We are not bodies and we are not souls, we are *embodied souls*. We are the invisible made visible. Think about that for a second. Our bodies are unique to the souls that they embody. Together, body and soul has a unique beauty, and a unique identity specific to that individual. Like a fingerprint, there are no two embodied souls that are identical. Your body is how other people are able to identify you, to come to know you and experience life with you. Your body is the way that you are able to reveal your soul and heart to those in this world that you love. It is a beautiful thing. You are a beautiful thing.

When we forget this and separate our hearts and souls from our bodies, we start to judge our bodies as mere objects. We start to see our bodies as pieces that are broken or imperfect, with parts that we wish we could exchange.

If we are doing this to our own bodies, it makes it that much easier for men to do so as well. As we grow up, most of the attention we come to long for is from men, especially as we hit puberty and those hormones start to kick in. We discover that the beauty of our bodies is one way we can begin to get this attention. We wear certain clothes and makeup to help us achieve the ideal images of beauty in hopes of attracting men. The problem is that we are using our bodies—not our personalities or our hearts—as objects to seek that attention we desire. When a man looks at a woman and sees only her body, if that is the part of herself that she is revealing to him, he will objectify her as she has objectified herself. From there, it is easy for a man to sexualize her. Men are physical beings and can quickly make this jump when they see no depth in a woman, nothing beyond the clothes, the makeup, the curves—everything that was meant to attract them, but does so in a distorted, empty way.

This skewed physical attraction is seen in an extreme way in the high numbers of men addicted to pornography. Just as we women fear being told that we are not pretty enough, men fear being told that they are not good enough. Sometimes this fear leads to a fear of commitment or a fear of failing the women they come to love. Some men take these distorted attractions to women and fall captive to the temptation of pornography or masturbation, both of which allow them to appreciate the physical beauty of women and the pleasure it can bring them without having to commit, to pursue, or to give of themselves in any way. About 64 to 68 percent of young adult men and about 18 percent of women use porn at least once every week.[5] We hadn't realized just how big a problem this is in our world, or how many men wrestle with it, until we got to college and made friends with guys who shared their struggles with each of us. And these were good men! Good men fallen captive to the objectification and sexualization of women, just as us women have, but in a different way.

We are taught to be the objects; men are taught to desire and acquire these objects. In both cases, though, objectifying the body is harming our capacity as individuals and as a society to see one another for more. It has altered our ability to truly get to know those around us, their hearts, their personalities, their souls—not just the surface-level masks that people are willing to let others see.

Another problem we face in our largely sexualized culture is that the objectification of women teaches men to seek the fake beauty of the Photoshopped and fantasized women in the pictures they are seeing—pictures that have created a standard of beauty in their minds that we real women can't meet. Then when we fall for these men, we find ourselves fighting an impossible battle against fake women to keep the attention of the men we love. All the while we are still caught in the mind-set of having to be the most beautiful in order to win them.

But women, what do you really want to captivate, a man's eyes or *his heart*? You get to choose by the way you present yourself, by the kind of beauty that you decide to reveal to the world. We can defeat this objectification and sexualization in our lives by first ceasing to objectify ourselves. Look in the mirror and see you—all of you. Then help the men around you to do the same. Recognize your beauty for what it is, all encompassing; and make *that* the beauty you embody every day.

3. Self-Negativity and Harm (Megan)

Objectification of our bodies is not easily defeated, though. We begin looking at our body as imperfect and in need of alterations from a very early age. Even when you think you are having a good day, society will always do you the favor of showing you something else that's wrong with you or something about yourself that you need to fix. This unending negativity can lead to misguided and harmful behavioral choices.

Remember in the beginning of the book we asked you to look in the mirror and think about what you saw? It's disheartening to know that the vast majority of women are trained to see faults first when we look in the mirror. It's like some sort of sick reflex we can't control. In fact, many studies have found a link between exposure to the "thin ideal" in mass media, and body dissatisfaction and internalization of this thin ideal resulting in disordered eating habits in women.[13] It's heartbreaking to see the effects that growing up in our society has had on our self-image. We fixate on our imperfections and strive for an unrealistic ideal that can at times have devastating consequences. Even the most seemingly confident and beautiful woman can so easily point out dozens of flaws before a single genuine self-compliment. It's true what they say, that *comparison is the thief of joy*. When we focus on comparing ourselves to others, no one wins. We search for flaws in the person next to us to tear them down in order to build ourselves up. If we find them to be better than us, we tear ourselves down in defeat and feel that we aren't good enough. The most important thing to remember about these comparisons is that no matter which way they sway, in your favor or not, they are a *lie*. Your beauty does not exist because of how it compares to the beauty of another woman. It exists separately and uniquely, as does hers.

I've experienced the effects of these negative thoughts in my own life, and I know I'm not the only one. In high school, like so many others I fell into the trap of comparison. I saw beautiful women in magazines and on TV and I wanted to be beautiful like them. I craved being skinny and desired. I felt myself create this bond between thinness and beauty that I couldn't separate. Then I began comparing myself to other women around me—my friend with the thigh gap and muscular legs, my classmate with the flat stomach and big boobs, my sisters with the naturally perfect figures, and girls who were shorter or smaller. I wanted what they had, and I decided to do whatever it took to get it. I began to work out to an unhealthy extreme. When that didn't give me the immediate response I wanted, I tried not eating. Food, I thought, was the real problem keeping me from being thin. I began passing out, and when friends and family started to catch on I realized that I needed to eat to keep up appearances, but no one could force me to keep down what I ate. I was going to be skinny at any cost—and then I would be beautiful and desirable.

Too many women struggle with feeling worthless and undesired. These feelings lead to self-harm, depression, or eating disorders; which are real and saddening consequences of the world we live in. The cost of "beauty" in our world is too high. I wish I could go back in time and shake myself out of that phase. I was blessed with good friends who built me back up again before I fell into a hole I couldn't have gotten out of without serious help. I was lucky. However, some women find themselves in these situations and aren't able to find the help they need. It's scary to accept the fact that eating disorders cause more deaths than any other mental disorder.[14]

We are self-destructive; we cut, starve, push ourselves to the limit, and for what? To find ourselves standing in front of the bathroom mirror crying over our appearance, because we still don't fit society's misperception of beauty. I can tell you right now that I don't and I never will fit society's definition of beauty, but I won't let that define me anymore. I am beautiful for one reason and one alone: because I am HIS. I'm a freaking princess because my Father is the King! And that realization is what changed things for me right there. It wasn't easy, but through prayer and the support of great friends I came to find what I hope that everyone who has ever felt the way I did discovers: you are sacred, you are treasured, you are wanted, you are His. So *please*, if this is you, ask for help. Asking for help is not a sign of weakness, it's a sign of strength. Start somewhere, anywhere—a friend, your mom, a school counselor, someone you trust. Don't stay silent. You are not alone, so don't let yourself feel isolated. Your life is worth the fight it will take to regain your health.

Negative body image is real and toxic. It can spread like a disease and cloud our minds to the truth: that each woman is a beautiful and unique creation of God. We are created in His image and with His essence. But in this day and age, we respond all too eagerly to the demands of society to be or act a certain way. It's so easy to fall victim to the cycle of self-negativity. We see our flaws and failings first. We forget to see our own beauty. It's extremely difficult as a woman to be able to stare in a mirror and not zero in on our thunder thighs, muffin top, or facial flaws.

However, what we see as "flaws" aren't really flaws at all. They make up who you are as a woman, and believe me, you're the only one dwelling on them. If it were your best friend staring back at you what would you tell her? Surely at least a dozen compliments would pop into your mind. Why can't we show this same kindness to our own bodies?

Those thunder thighs are just a part of the wicked curves that make up your hourglass figure. Your bloated stomach means that your body is working the way it should; women get a little extra around the middle, it's just how we're created! We are made to bear life and life needs nutrients to grow from. It's beautiful! And those facial flaws you notice are characteristics that make up the face that God has given you, a unique face that allows others to recognize you as solely you. They are not flaws. They are your eyes that glow when you're excited and your smile that lights up a room and brings joy to others. *That* is what others see when they look at you. You are not flawed. You are a unique, artistic creation. You are a beautiful daughter of the King. You are more than enough.

However, this is so difficult for us as women to grasp because we are constantly taught otherwise. So the solution then lies in breaking these habits, redirecting our eyes and thoughts, and transforming the images we have of ourselves—no simple task, we know. The first time the two of us were able to even approach this topic together was over a midcollege, end of summer, all-you-can-eat sushi dinner. Let me tell you, it's not easy to feel all that beautiful while you're gorging yourself with nigiri and rainbow rolls, but we made a decision that day to love ourselves and respect our bodies in a whole new way. Moving forward from that night we have had to continue making that decision *every single day.*

Why is it so natural for women to receive a compliment and immediately retort with a reason why it isn't true? "No, you're wrong. These pants don't look good on me, they make me look fat." "I don't look pretty, I have bags under my eyes and my hair's a mess." *"You're wrong, that compliment can't be true."*

Why do we do that? That is not only unkind to our bodies but also disrespectful to the person giving us a genuine compliment. However, to be able to recognize what others see as beautiful in us we first must be able to see our own beauty. *We choose what we see in the mirror.* That night at sushi, we realized we were too fixated on our flaws and decided to make a change in the way we view our own bodies. We could then:

* Allow ourselves to see that we are beautiful
* Accept the beauty others see in us
* Turn around and recognize the beauty in other women without envy, but with genuine appreciation for one another

4. Beauty Exercises

To begin incorporating these three key points in our lives, we came up with these beauty exercises. We now challenge you to do the same tasks. What we are asking of you is not easy or comfortable at first, but if we can do it so can you. Grab a great girlfriend (or a few) and give this a shot. You can hold each other accountable and validate each other in ways that will help you appreciate your beautiful selves. Make the choice and make the change. No girlfriends around? Do it for yourself.

A. LOVE THE BODY GOD GAVE YOU
For this first part, each girl must list at least five genuine compliments about her own physical beauty. We aren't looking for "Oh, I have a nice personality." Nah girl, you have some killer legs, or stunning blue eyes! Appreciate what the good Lord and your Mama gave you!

B. ACCEPT COMPLIMENTS FROM OTHERS
It's easy to list dozens of compliments about how beautiful a good friend of yours looks, so here is your chance. Now give each other five genuine compliments about physical beauty, as you did for yourself. Here's the catch though: you each have to *accept* these compliments. That's right. No disagreeing or negating. Accept, absorb, and appreciate the beauty others see in you. Pay it forward and return the favor to others.

C. DAILY CHOOSE TO SEE YOURSELF AS BEAUTIFUL
Every day you will have to make the choice to do this on your own; but girlfriends are always great to hold you accountable and give you reminders. Take what you see as beautiful in yourself and what others see as beautiful in you and carry it with you throughout your day. Post it on your mirror, keep it on your cell phone screen, or put a little reminder in your car. If you are doing this with friends then text each other little reminders that you are beautiful exactly as you are—as God has created you to be. Here's a few examples of what we placed in planners, on mirrors, in our cars, and on our phones as reminders:

* "She is clothed in strength and dignity and laughs without fear of the future."—Proverbs 31:25
* "Promise me you'll always remember you are braver than you believe, stronger than you seem, and smarter than you think."—Christopher Robin
* "Dear Lord, when feelings of inferiority, insecurity, and self-doubt creep into my heart, help me to see myself the way You do."—Anonymous Pinterest quote
* "You are altogether beautiful my love, there is no flaw in you."—Song of Solomon 4:7
* Insert practically any Audrey Hepburn quote here. Here's one of our favorites: "Elegance is the only beauty that never fades."

You can even turn these reminders into a fun crafting activity with friends! Make a cute canvas or picture frame. If you're completely devoid of creative abilities like us, just write it on a bunch of Post-its or print something off the computer. Whatever it takes to remind yourself that you are uniquely beautiful, do it. At the same time, start making a conscious effort to give yourself and other women *genuine* compliments. For example, instead of saying "That dress looks great on you," say "You look great in that dress." See the difference? The first way, you're saying something nice about the dress that can easily and too often turn into "Thanks . . . it's not mine," or "Yeah, I got it on sale." The second way, you're saying something nice about the person. The dress may be great, but it's you or your friend who makes it beautiful. It's a small change that makes a big difference.

Ladies, when it comes down to it, *we* get to choose what the mirror reflects, not society. Throw away the lies that you aren't enough. You are more than enough and you are wonderfully made by a Father who cherishes you. He knows everything about you—every clumsy moment, "bad hair day," or moment that you may regret—and He loves you more than you can imagine. We are each a masterpiece that He created, so who are we to critique such a work of art?

The battle for true beauty begins within. What do you see in the mirror now?

5. Living Out Our Beauty (Kaylin)

My priest once shared a simple but powerful piece of advice with me after I told him about my struggles with judging myself and comparing myself to others. He told me to say this prayer, which is based on a quote from C. S. Lewis:

> Lord, help me to never think *less of myself*, but *of myself less*.

This simple prayer unlocked for me the secret to inner freedom that I had been longing for. To explain to you how such a short phrase was able to accomplish such a feat, let me break the prayer into two halves.

The first part of this prayer, the "help me to never think less of myself" part, encompasses everything we have been talking about so far in this book. It is a reminder that we are beautiful, and that believing we are not is a dangerous and slippery slope. When we devalue ourselves we open the door for others to do so as well. We have been carefully created by a Father who loves each of us individually. Stop for a moment and think about what this means.

The Creator of the ocean, its great depth and color and power; the Creator of the universe, every planet and falling star; the Creator of every creature, from the colorful hummingbird to the majestic horse; that same Creator created *you*. And He set you apart from this already alluring symphony of beauty and life by creating you last. You are the pinnacle, the *crown* of all His creation. The beauty of creation escalated each day until you, the *woman,* adorned it all.

> Thus the heavens and the earth were completed in all their vast array . . . Then the Lord God formed a man from the dust of the ground and breathed into his nostrils the breath of life, and the man became a living being . . . So the man gave names to all the livestock, the birds in the sky and all the wild animals. But for Adam no suitable helper was found . . . Then the Lord God made a woman from the rib he had taken out of the man, and he brought her to the man.—Genesis 1:1, 7, 20, 22

God created nothing new on earth after woman; and there is nothing more inherently beautiful. That means that even a beautiful crimson and gold sun setting behind the outline of the Rocky Mountains ain't got nothing on us! What gives the sun its strength or the rose its beauty? Is it because it wakes up and says, today I will choose to shine brighter, or bend this petal to appear more attractive? No, it doesn't need to, because its creator has already instilled beauty into the creation itself. Our beauty does not lie in what we wear or what makeup we apply. We wake up beautiful simply because we are *created* beautiful—just like the rose.

Now I'm not saying that we should all just roll out of bed, run out of the house, and tell the world to bask in our beauty (drool-stained, crazy hair, leftover mascara and all). No, that might be a bit much. What I am saying is that we need to recognize our beauty from the second we wake up until the second we go to sleep. When we forget, we need to say a short prayer to ask God to allow us to see ourselves through His adoring eyes—the eyes of a proud Father gazing with love at His beautiful little girl.

After we've started our day this way, reminding ourselves how beautiful we are, *then* we can go about putting on our clothes and maybe even some makeup to enhance our natural beauty. It's not bad that we are drawn to pretty things; it only becomes a problem when we excessively rely on them, hide behind them, or place our self-worth or beauty in them. It is the same thing as eating well or exercising. Taking care of our bodies is a great thing as long as we are not motivated by negative self-thoughts. Take care of yourself, but do it because *you are worth it*, not because you feel you aren't.

This leads to the second half of the short prayer, the "think of myself less" part. This is the understated but oh-so-important key to the freedom we are searching for. It is this part that allows us to start living out our beauty and sharing it with the world.

Think about it, when is it that we judge ourselves? When do we compare ourselves to another woman sitting next to us, or the model on the cover of a magazine? When do we fidget with our clothes, or glance in horror at a mirror as we frantically fix our hair or makeup? It is when, and only when, *we are thinking about ourselves*. I know, I know, it seems obvious; but I'm serious. The moment that we stop thinking, "What do I look like right now? What are they thinking of me?" and start thinking, "How can I make this person smile? How can I do something to make that person feel loved?" then you are free! All of a sudden it's not about you; it's about what you are doing, it's about the person that you're with, and it's about living life and being present. Suddenly you have captured your inner beauty and are sharing it with the world and those around you. Now *that* is a beauty you will be remembered for, a beauty that is lasting, inspiring, and contagious.

By thinking less about ourselves and thinking more about how we can make a difference in the lives of those around us, we become beautiful in the way that we were created to be. True beauty leads others to feel loved and beautiful, and gives them a taste of the presence of something divine in our world. By doing this, our beauty finds its original purpose and depth.

We are called to go out and share our beauty with the world and in doing so to nurture the lives of those we meet. However, we must remember that in order to do this we must first recognize that this beauty exists within us, and allow our Creator to remind us when we forget.

If a sunset can make people stop in awe and can fill their hearts with joy, how much more can our relatable, nurturing, joyful, life-filled beauty bring to others? You are God's unique *gift* to this world. It is time to start allowing yourself to believe that.

PART II
What Is Modesty?

❧

1. THE GREAT MYSTERY

NOW THAT WE HAVE A greater understanding of beauty, we are going to take a look at how we can best share our all-encompassing beauty with a primarily physical-focused world.

Let's go back to the "embodied souls" idea touched on in the last part. This idea was the focus of Pope St. John Paul II's Theology of the Body, which he spoke on and compiled during his papacy in order to remind the world of the great dignity of the human person and the beauty of our sexuality as man and woman. The main theme of these lectures, letters, and now book, the pope said, was that "the body, and it alone, is capable of making visible what is invisible: the spiritual and the divine. It was created to transfer into the visible reality of the world, the mystery hidden since time immemorial in God, and thus to be a sign of it."[28]

Our bodies are the visible, tangible, representation of who we are and all that we are, but also of the great mystery of our Creator Himself. This is no small matter. In the creation of the physical world, God distinguished humanity from all else because:

> God created mankind in his own image, in the image of
> God he created them; male and female he created them.
> —Genesis 1:27

Sometimes it is easy to feel like life is all about chasing the next shiny object, the newest fad, or the coolest iPhone. However, even dogs chase shiny cars, so why do only humans wonder if we are made for more? Maybe it's because we *are*. We have been set apart from the rest of creation. God chose to reveal Himself intimately to the world through humanity, through each of us.

Just like children reveal different aspects of their parents in a way that is unique to each child, so do we reveal different aspects of our Father. One way we reveal our Father is through our sexuality: our masculinity and femininity. Through men, God reveals Himself to be a protector, a warrior, a stronghold, a leader, and a Father. Through women, He reveals Himself to be loving, nurturing, communal, life-giving, and *beautiful*. We long to be sought after, pursued, and delighted in because God longs for humanity to seek Him, pursue Him, and delight in Him. We are beautiful because God is so incredibly beautiful, beyond all comprehension—and in us the world glimpses that beauty.

He has given us an amazing gift, a chance to come to know Him more through those around us. Even by the fact that we are made male and female, biologically compatible to become one and drawn to do so, we see God's own communal aspect of the Trinity. Three persons: Father, Son, and Holy Spirit, and yet one God. This is similar to how man and wife become one, through love, through their sexuality, and a third person, a child, is born to embody that love. (We will discuss this aspect of our sexuality more in Part III.)

So men and women reveal pieces of God to the world, but we are not the only way that God chose to reveal Himself. God also came to us in Jesus Christ. God Himself became human—one of us, His mere creations. Why would He do this? What does it mean? By examining answers to these questions we can discover different aspects of what it means to reveal God to the world as women.

Before Christ came into the world, God was still God; but to most humans He was strictly the Creator and the all-powerful, all-knowing King. In our humanity we had no idea how to relate to Him; He seemed to be distant and beyond understanding.

This gap in understanding occurred because soon after we were created we became selfish and used our gift of *free will*—given to us so that we could *choose*, an act that is necessary for genuine love—to try to grasp life for ourselves, when God was trying to offer it to us as a gift. We broke our relationship with God, our provider, in the name of independence, and in doing so created this distance from Him. Have you ever seen a sassy teenager do this? Yeah, it wasn't the last time we've used our independence selfishly. Sin and selfishness entered the world and unfortunately are very much alive today. God continued to love us immensely, as parents do even when their child misbehaves, but He had to watch as we continued to hurt Him by our choices and to block Him from our lives. Finally, out of His love for us, He sent us His only Son, Jesus Christ, to live with us and to die for us—to remind us what love truly means.

The fall of humanity and the mystery of the Incarnation, God becoming man, are important concepts to grasp before we can discuss the mystery of feminine beauty. In humanity's fallen state we were not able to see God for all that He is. We were unsure of His love for us, of His will for our lives, of why He even created us, and unsure of how to approach Him. Through Jesus Christ, God chose to *veil* His majesty, His power, His divinity, His beauty, so that we could learn these things in a way that we could understand. He came as a baby, born to a young girl and raised by her and a carpenter in Bethlehem. He walked this Earth, experiencing life as we do, all so that He could show us life as it was meant to be. By doing this He also showed us the

secret to love: a total gift of self, a sacrifice that we had long forgotten. He restored the path to a relationship with God through
His death and Resurrection, and reminded us what it means to
love one another here on Earth as well.

God was able to do all of this through the Incarnation because of one key component: *the flesh part.* If God had not veiled
Himself with human flesh, we could not have related to Him.
We would have been unable to see what He was trying to show
us. It is similar for us, as women. Our physical beauty, which is a
wonderful aspect of who we are, must be *veiled* so that our fallen
world can see our true beauty within.

Think about it. Let's say you see a girl next to you in class
and she is absolutely beautiful. She has long, perfectly curled
hair, striking blue eyes outlined in black, and a tight crop top
with mini jean shorts that show off her perfect model body.
What's the first thing you would think? "I wonder if she has a
big heart?" "She looks so welcoming. I would love to get to know
her." "I wonder what her passions and dreams are?" No, probably
not. And she may have the biggest heart in the world! But unfortunately that is not the beauty that she is choosing to broadcast
to the world. Even as a woman I would be slightly distracted by
her choice of clothes if I was talking to her. Imagine how much
harder it would be for a man. Remember the "Women as Sex
Objects" section? Men are already visual beings created with a
natural attraction to us. We are made to be especially beautiful
to them, which is a good thing.

However, with the fall of humanity, everything as it was
made to be has become distorted—and that includes this attraction to beauty. Now, this attraction to women can quickly

lead them to strip us of our dignity with their eyes, making us an object of fantasy or sexual desire in their minds, even if they don't initially intend this. For the men who want to feed off their sexual fantasies, it becomes much easier for them to do so if we choose to display our bodies and leave little to the imagination, compromising our own mystery. As we discussed earlier, this distortion has also caused shockingly high rates of addiction to pornography and masturbation, and it is not just women online that they use, it's women they see—it's *us*, even if they don't know us.

If a man was trying to talk to the woman described above, he would either be choosing to sexualize her or fighting hard not to. I doubt that she truly wants that response. Her physical beauty is a great thing, but by choosing to make that the focus of how she presents herself to the world, she is robbing herself of the love and respect she is truly seeking and instead is getting merely the attention she is asking for—maybe unknowingly. Even if she is well aware of the kind of attention she is asking for, I have yet to meet one woman who can truly look at me and say, "What I really want more than anything in the world is to be wanted for my body. I don't care if anyone actually knows me on a deeper level and loves me for me." That simply cannot be true; it's not how we were made. We are women. We love *love*! We crave to be loved for *who we are* and to be seen as beautiful exactly *as we are*.

This is where the veil comes in. By veiling our bodies, as sacred items were veiled in a temple and as God veiled Himself in Jesus, we remind both ourselves and others of the sacredness of our beauty and invite them to come to know our hearts first.

2. The Triple Threat

The most important way that we veil our beauty is through *modesty*. The definition of modesty as found in the dictionary is "behavior, manner, or appearance intended to avoid impropriety or indecency."[25] Wait, what? Isn't modesty just about dressing like a prude in long skirts and turtlenecks? No. I mean if you like long skirts and turtlenecks go for it! But that's not usually our first outfit choice! Modesty is actually so much more than that; it involves a triple threat. The key to being the beautifully modest women we are called to be lies in the way we *dress*, *act* and *speak*.

A. *Dress* for Dignity, Not Society (Megan)

"You don't get it. That guy over there, he lives in my dorm. He's addicted to porn. And you know what he sees when he looks at you or any other woman in those legging pants? He sees the perfect form of whatever porn star body he wants, the ones that he spends his free time looking at, to pop in over your body. I know you think it doesn't matter but it does. I don't want you to be thought of like that. Don't dress like this. To you it's just for comfort, but for some guys? It's free porn."

"Leggings? She wants me to see her figure, right? And I can. I mean, it hugs her whole butt and the fabric is practically see-through."

"Guys don't really narrate it much but if you're at the pool and you see a girl in a tiny bikini bottom, for example, one guy may point to her butt and the rest will look. But nothing needs to be said, everyone is thinking the same thing."

"Strapless dresses push up plenty and show off the breasts, that's what they're for. But also many guys can't help but think that they would be really easy to pull down or off."

"Girls constantly adjust [strapless tops], which draws your attention right back to their breasts."

"Halloween has the best parties because the girls dress really slutty! And if she's dressed slutty, it translates to guys that she would be more willing to get with him."

What you just read are quotes straight from the mouths of college men. We talked to a variety of them, from fraternity guys to solid Catholic men, and do you know who they are talking about in these quotes? *You.* Wearing things like leggings and yoga pants, bikinis, and strapless or short dresses. We know; we were shocked at first, too. We always hear how visual guys are, but until you hear it like this, you just don't get it. They don't know your name but they know your every curve, whether you want them to or not. If they catch a glimpse of you bending over to unlock your bike or pick up your books they could tell you what color of underwear you're wearing; but they couldn't tell you the color of your eyes. They can mentally undress you in seconds if they choose to and they know exactly how to fill in the blanks (with whatever they want) on *your* body. Is this what you want to be thought of walking to class, the bus, or your car?

Obviously much of the problem here lies in the heart of the man entertaining such thoughts and the habits that lead him to these thoughts. Degrading words and thoughts that have been used by a man toward you are *never* your fault. Ever. You deserve respect from all men at all times no matter what, simply because of the dignity that you inherently possess. However, we as women can make conscious clothing choices to protect ourselves in a world where some men do choose these thoughts. We also need to remember that our physical beauty also distracts good men when we choose to reveal it so blatantly to them; it is not just the jerks you may be picturing in your head right now. Carefully choosing our clothing is for our sake and for the sake of the good men in our life whom we want to help fight this battle.

This book is not for men, so we will not address the underlying issue that exists in some of these quotes; instead we will focus on what we as women can do while living in such a world. How can we dress to reveal our dignity and not just our body parts—and look beautiful while doing it? This is the big question we are going to look at now.

First of all, ladies, we have bad news: leggings are not pants. They are *tights*. They're barely another layer of skin. It took us awhile to come to terms with this news as well. I mean, they're so comfortable and easy to wear! They may be great for around the house but we really do have to start wearing some real pants in public. When we both decided to stop wearing leggings we had to face the sad reality that we no longer owned any other kind of pants. We fixed this by starting with some comfy black jeans that would still go with everything. And once you get some pants—taking that extra few seconds in the morning to zip and button—soon you won't be able to imagine wearing anything else.

It wasn't until one of my best guy friends repeatedly asked me to stop wearing leggings that it finally hit me and I realized that leggings aren't supposed to be worn in public on their own. He told me what some good guys we know think when they see tight clothing like that and it made me sick to my stomach. What he told me is the first quote in the list above, about a guy I personally knew using my body as "free porn." I appreciate my friend more than he can know for continuing to tell me this until it finally clicked. I want to be thought of with more dignity than that and it's my responsibility to dress in a manner that demands respect. Yes, men have the responsibility to guard their thoughts, but it's a two-way street. We need to return the favor to men by dressing in a way that doesn't simplify our bodies to an object of desire. We are so much more than that! We have a responsibility to protect our hearts by protecting our bodies from being used or thought of in that way. Pants are a small price to pay for that.

A big part of what the men are saying in the quotes above is that it's all about accessibility. How accessible are you making your body in the way you dress? Wearing bikinis is practically walking around naked, but in a more perfected way. Strapless dresses are just waiting to fall off, and before they do we tug on them to hold them in place, which, as one of the men said, draws even more attention to our breasts. Leggings and yoga pants leave nothing to the imagination. Low-cut shirts distract from your beautiful pair of eyes, to another pair you'll be frustrated to find is all men can look at when you talk to them in those clothes. We're already just so naturally gorgeous, geez, let's not make it even more difficult for men to focus by flinging body parts at them to distract them from a real conversation.

So what about the classic: "It's my body and I can dress the way I want." Well, yes, you can; but what kind of message are you sending to those around you? What kind of woman are you telling the world you are every day you walk out the door? *Be the woman who shows how beautiful she is without showing everything.* Our bodies are worth the extra effort it takes to dress in a modest manner. We are beautiful and part of that beauty lies in the mystery of our bodies. It is not beautiful to be hanging out of our clothes every which way. Society often tells us otherwise, and it's not easy when it seems like everyone else is following the crowd and you're standing on your own. However, it's worth it to take an extra step to be noticed for the right reasons; and trust us, you're *not* standing alone in this decision.

We both spent a good amount of time wearing and loving the leggings with oversized sweaters and boots look. We got new bikinis every summer and we wore the short and strapless dresses; but we never felt comfortable with so much of our bodies exposed and didn't understand why. When we got the whistles or the double looks we were asking for from guys, we started to realize that we really didn't want that. The more we learned about dressing modestly, the more it continued to resonate with us as something we wanted. We realized that it would be a challenge to go against the norms of society and *gasp!* actually cover ourselves; but we had to follow our hearts. Not just for those around us, but for our own confidence and comfort.

It began with this idea, which then led to discussions, which culminated in a complete wardrobe overhaul. And it is this exact overhaul that we now recommend to you, to help you make that change and commit to veiling your beautiful body as you deserve. It's an all-in/ all-out kind of thing, so don't think you can do this halfway. We tried that, too, and it never works. So either on your own or with your great solid girlfriends, challenge yourself to: *The Closet Overhaul.*

Step 1: Talk it out. Grab a friend and some good coffee and decide what kind of message you want to send with your clothes. Figure out what looks good on your body type. There is no "one size fits all." What brings out your best features and covers you?

Step 2: The closet. With your friend or your incredible will-power, go through your entire closet—the whole thing. Try it all on, and your friend gets to tell you whether it stays or goes modesty wise. To help you decide, ask yourselves these questions:

- Does it actually cover me?
- Is it flattering? Do I feel beautiful/confident in it?
- Can I move without anything falling out of weird places?
- Bend over. Can you see too much leg, butt, or boobs?
- If another woman was wearing this in front of my future husband, would I be okay with that?

Remember that if you really have to ask if it's modest, it most likely isn't. Trust your gut and be honest with yourself. When we did this we each lost two garbage bags worth of clothes. No joke. It wasn't easy. All but two gym shorts didn't make the cut, lots of dresses disappeared, and unflattering, low-cut shirts got added to the donation pile. But the best part is that now when we go to pick out an outfit we don't have to think about whether it will be modest enough or if we will look good and feel good in it. Everything in our closets is cute, flattering, and makes us feel confident in our own skin. Now *that* is a great feeling.

Step 3: Shop until you drop! (Maybe literally.) Shopping for clothes that are fashionable, fit your body type, and cover you is next to impossible but it is doable! Even if it's a lot easier to find a dress that would pass as a shirt than it is to find one that goes to your knees and is cute at the same time, they do exist. It just takes time, patience and commitment. Always remember, "Your clothes should be tight enough to show you're a woman, but loose enough to show you're a lady" (Marilyn Monroe). We did it and so can you. If you aren't a big shopper, try online shopping! (Visit our website with more tips, tricks, and links about clothing and shopping.)

The more effort we each put into dressing modestly, the more modestly we wanted to dress. We can all rise to the challenge of dressing well because it feels good to be noticed for who we are, not just for what our bodies look like. Nothing feels better than rocking your day in a great outfit that makes you feel confident and beautiful without having to worry about what you are causing guys or other women around you to think. Then any compliments are just gravy on top.

Dressing modestly in our world today is hard. If you haven't noticed, it's not exactly the most popular choice. It would definitely be easier to throw on the leggings or little dress and fit in with the college and high school world we live in, but we are called to more than that. We are mysterious and others are drawn to us for what lies within, not for what body parts we show off. The men around you will be grateful for your efforts; the women around you will see that you have a confidence in your dress that encourages them to make the same effort. Best of all, you will feel more confident and beautiful in your own skin.

> "When a girl cares about dressing modestly it really shows a love for her brothers in Christ and an awareness of the struggle that occurs on a daily basis."
> —Male college student

B. *Act* Like the Lady You Are

Now that we have a better understanding of how to *dress* like the beautiful ladies that we are, we need to look at how to *act* like a lady. Remember that scene in *The Princess Diaries* when Queen Clarisse (Julie Andrews) is teaching Mia (Anne Hathaway) to be a princess? Princesses don't slump around; they stand up straight and walk tall. They present their best self to the world and so should we. Perhaps our crowns got lost in the mail or something, but we still want to act like the royalty we are. The King has given us the title—now we just have to show it!

People respond to the way we act much more than we realize. In fact, more than 80 percent of communication is nonverbal.[26] This means that the people around us see how we behave and make quick judgments based on our behavior. So stand tall, sit like a lady, be poised and confident, and show the world what kind of woman you are. Most importantly: *Be yourself!* If you're super sporty, own it. Girly girl, bring on the glitter and glam. Hipster chick, rock the plaid and Birkenstocks. Don't try to fit a mold of the perfect woman, be the perfect woman you are with class, dignity, and self-respect.

It's true what they say that actions speak louder than words. So "Live your life in such a way that if someone were to speak badly of you, no one would believe it" (Anonymous Pinterest quote). This doesn't mean be proper and prim at all times, it means be classy and beautiful *you*—however that may apply. You are a unique creation of God; so let your true, beautiful self shine through. Don't fall into the trap of society pressuring you to act in a way that compromises your dignity; you're worth more than that. Respect those around you and inspire them to respect you through your actions and how you live your life.

C. THINK BEFORE YOU *SPEAK* (MEGAN)

How you dress and act mean nothing if your words don't match up. It's like Thumper said in the movie *Bambi*, "If you can't say anything nice, don't say nothing at all." One of the most important struggles many of us face is the temptation to use curse words or to swear. I used to cuss like a sailor to fit in with the people I surrounded myself with. It leaked into my life to the point that the F-word became a sentence filler. Attractive, huh? It's really not. I'm sad to say that cussing is something I still struggle with because I let it become a habit and habits are very difficult to break. It's a daily challenge for me to speak like a lady, not a sailor on leave. So flip-flop, gosh dang it, I'm going to keep pushing myself until this habit is broken because cussing is tacky and that is not the image of myself I want to portray to those around me. What are your words saying about you?

One good way to watch what you say is to watch what you let into your mind. Thoughts become words, especially for us women—we are good at the talking thing. So watch what music you listen to, the degrading or dirty jokes you encourage, and the movies you watch and end up quoting. All these things become a part of you and they definitely become a part of your vocabulary.

I was on a date one time with a really great guy. It was the typical dinner-and-movie date, but he had bought the movie tickets based on the time rather than what was playing, so we had no idea what we were walking into. We thought it would be a fun surprise that way, but the main surprise was seeing the kind of language and content allowed on the big screen! Barely fifteen minutes into the movie he and I were completely uncomfortable and I couldn't bring myself to laugh with the crowd at the inappropriate humor on the screen. Instead of going with the crowd this time, as I had done countless times before, I turned to my date and told him I couldn't watch this movie. We quickly left the theater and just as I was going to apologize for being such a prude and wasting the tickets, *he thanked me*. He was grateful that I was the kind of girl to leave the theater instead of laughing along. I was shocked! Good men will actually appreciate women who ask them to raise their standards. Men naturally love to be challenged and when we challenge them, we help them to become the men they want to be.

> To a great extent the level of any civilization is the level of its womanhood. When a man loves a woman, he has to become worthy of her. The higher her virtue, the more noble her character, the more devoted she is to truth, justice, and goodness, the more a man has to aspire to be worthy of her. The history of civilization could actually be written in terms of the level of its women.—Archbishop Fulton J. Sheen

My date in particular spent the rest of the night bragging to practically every person we ran into about me and how we left the movie because we weren't the kind of people who want to watch something like that. He still talks about it and thanks me to this day. What we watch and listen to truly does speak to our character; and true men appreciate and respect a woman of character.

As we discussed earlier, how we respond to compliments and nice things that others do for us also distinguishes us as speaking like ladies. I've had so many guys tell me how much it hurts them when a woman yells at them for opening the door for them. Our words and actions can discourage men from being gentlemen! Why the heck would we want to do that?

One guy told me that in high school he really liked this girl, so he got her flowers because they were pretty and reminded him of her beauty. He was so excited as he walked up to give them to her, but what did she do? She laughed at him and mocked him for being cheesy. Men naturally want to serve and do things to show us that they like us. When we shut them down or hurt them with our words, we create the very men that we then come to detest. We are supposed to inspire them to be gentlemen, not stop them. Let men do things for you. Yes, that is hard at first because we are stubborn and independent and fully capable. But by doing it, we are helping men be gentlemen, and therefore helping ourselves.

One final thing that we women need to work on in order to speak like ladies is gossip. Gossiping is everywhere—at school, at coffee shops, at sleepovers, and in the hallways, and it needs to stop. We are not saying that it is a bad thing to get your friend's opinion on something or to seek help when you are in a sticky situation; seeking wise advice is a great thing! However, tearing others down or simply speaking poorly of them so that you have something to talk about is never okay. Be the woman who no one has ever heard speak poorly of another person and who is kind with her words. One tip is to try leaving out names when you seek advice so that you don't say something that could diminish another person's reputation. If you give up gossip and find yourself lacking topics of conversation, this is the perfect opportunity to learn how to truly ask about the heart of the person you are with and see how they are doing. It is never too late to relearn the art of genuine conversation.

We think Audrey Hepburn perfectly summarizes this section on modesty in her famous quote:

For beautiful eyes, look for the good in others.
For beautiful lips, speak only words of kindness.
And for poise, walk with the knowledge that you are never alone

Does your beauty lie in the world or in something greater within? Let your dress, words, and actions lead you to be(you)tiful you so that everyone around you can see you for who you truly are.

PART III

Relationships

1. Prince Charming (Kaylin)

Growing up my favorite movie was *Cinderella*. I stared at the screen as Prince Charming swept her off her feet and they ran out smiling to the sound of wedding bells. I was all of two feet tall and four years old and I didn't know why the story, and any other like it, mesmerized me, but it just did. I'm willing to bet that many of you can relate to this. I mean, why do you think that chick flicks make the big bucks? It is most likely not because every guy is rushing to see its unpredictable plotline and nail-biting action; because let's be honest, chick flicks rarely contain either of those things. We know exactly what's going to happen, but women naturally love the romance. We love to watch as a guy becomes captivated by a woman's beauty and pursues her despite all the obstacles in his path. We all watch with "Awwws" or even tears as he professes his deep love for her and whisks her away to *Happily Ever After*.

Why is this? It's because we automatically place ourselves in the female lead role. We long for a man to want us like that, too, and desire to be that one woman in a man's life who is the most treasured part of his world. It's simply how we are hardwired as women. Men want women, and women want to be wanted by men; it's pretty clear that we have a good Creator who thought all of this out. However, as we grow from girls to women, eventually reality gives us a wake-up call, more harshly for some than others, and we realize that this *Happily Ever After* may just be a thing for the storybooks. As a result, some of us will turn in anger to these stories and the "lies" they fill our minds with; but that does not mean that this desire goes away. We are then left with two choices: we can push the desire down and deny that it exists out of our anger, and claim that romance is cheesy and unrealistic; or we can recognize that this desire is there and that it is good, and come to a new and mature vision of the love and romance that we were created for.

It is true that love is not as simple, carefree, quick, mindless, and free of trials as Disney and chick flicks try to make it look. We know this and we see it every day. The guys in our classes, on modern TV shows, or in popular songs aren't exactly the Prince Charmings that we dreamed about. It is also no secret that practically half of the couples who get married get divorced. So with these bleak realities, does that mean we just give up? Or perhaps that we have to lower our standards in order to get a guy? Do we just submit to the idea that this is how the world is now and if we want to find love we better "get with the times"? Maybe. I know that some of us will. However, as surprising as it may seem, we do not *have* to do that; we *choose* to do that.

Between the two of us, we have taken very different paths from being those little girls staring up at a Disney movie to where we are now. We've pretty much taken the exact opposite paths, actually. So no matter where you are at in your life right now, which path you are on or have taken, we hope that through us sharing our stories you may come to understand your own path better. Please realize that despite what the devil may want you to think, you are not alone. It is never too late to make a change; become the woman you actually want to be and allow your hope to be restored. Yes, Disney is unrealistic, and yes, love is much more complicated than that; but the King *is* real and you are *His princess*. No matter what, He loves you, and if it is marriage that you are called to than it is a prince who He has planned for you; even if he doesn't come exactly when you want and he doesn't ride in on a white stallion.

2. "College and Never Been Kissed?" (Kaylin)

"Wait. You've never been kissed before?!" Great, they found out. This was not exactly the way I wanted to start off freshman year at a big public university with my new friends. Come on, like I had never heard that before? Or seen those shocked facial expressions? You would think I just told a group of children that Santa doesn't exist! Yes, that's right. I'm in college, I'm nineteen, and yes, I do actually like men, but no, *I've never kissed anyone.*

That's one way to quickly feel abnormal and weird. I wasn't ashamed of this fact about myself until I found people looking at me like I have two heads or heard them saying, "Come on! What are you waiting for? Go kiss someone. It's not like it's something special or anything." At a new school, trying to make new friends, and trying to figure out the whole "college thing," standing out like this was not on my to-do list. I already do not like drawing attention to myself, so all I said was, "Yeah, I don't know . . . I haven't met anyone I want to kiss I guess." I found myself struggling to defend my decision to save my kiss for the right man. The more I saw of the college social life—the "hookup culture," as it has been understandably deemed—I began to sincerely believe that I was the *only* girl who had never even been on a date, let alone kissed a guy. Looking around, I thought I had to be.

Even though it has only been a couple of years since that moment, which I still clearly remember despite the fact that it wasn't the first time I'd been asked that, I have learned a lot. Not only about relationships, guys, and yes, even kissing, but also about how to put into words that decision I had made for myself. Whether you can relate to me and are thinking, "Wait, I'm not alone?" or whether you relate better to the people who were asking me this question, I hope my story will give you a new perspective.

Let's back it up now. Growing up I experienced a lot with relationships, just maybe not like most people do. I first watched the divorce, annulment, and remarriages of my parents. Then I watched as my friends dated countless different types of guys. I watched as dating advanced from the somewhat innocent middle school hand-holding to a whole new level of complicated drama. I watched as my closest friends got caught in the webs, and listened as they cried and told me that they did things they never thought they'd do. I tried my best when they came to me for counsel and comforted them when they had their hearts broken. I experienced it all, too—just not personally. We all learn in different ways and, thanks to God, observing was enough for me to have seen enough to choose a different path.

Whether you experience it personally or not, choosing to swim upstream in a fast downward-flowing river is not easy. Every song, every movie, every conversation at school, every ad on TV . . . just about *everything* is focused on people being in relationships, good or bad. So you feel *great* about yourself when you aren't in one. There is incredible pressure in our society to be with someone, as if singleness is a disease! It has taken me some time to fully see this, but I could not be more grateful for the years I had being single. So to all the single ladies out there, I'm going to speak specifically to you real quick.

If you are single one thing you may hear a lot is: "Your standards are *way* too high. That is so unrealistic. You'll never find anyone." As if you didn't already have that worry about becoming an old cat lady constantly popping up in the back of your mind. However, this is one of the biggest lies that anyone will tell you or that you may try to tell yourself. Women should not lower their standards just to get a guy. We have to keep the standards that are important to us high and trust that the right man will rise to meet them. Sure, if you lower them then that will give you more options, but you're not looking for lots of guys—you are looking for *one*. If you compromise on your values or on things that are really important to you for any relationship you want to be in, then you will get a relationship alright but it won't be the one you want.

I encourage you to take some time to sit down and actually write out your core values, the things that are nonnegotiable in any future relationship. Now I'm not talking about "big biceps," "6'2," "star of the football team"; if those things happen, they happen, but that's not love and it won't make you happy in the long run. I'm talking about deep things. For me they were things like: a man of faith, a man who respects all women, a man with a sense of humor, a man who is a leader. Then when you find someone with the character traits you value, give the guy a chance and let God surprise you; if he isn't the exact man you have created in your mind, that's okay, because chances are this one's even better.

That leads to another big thing that you may be told if you are single: "Come on, just date him for a while, it's like practice, it doesn't matter if you don't like him." How does that even make sense? If you date someone you will end up either breaking up or getting married; that's it. So yes, give guys a chance, but only guys with your core traits. Do not date just any guy so that you have a boyfriend. One or both of you will end up with a broken heart if you already know fundamentally that you are not compatible. Don't let people talk you into "practicing" with relationships that you know will end as quickly as they begin.

As a single lady you may also hear countless comments directed at you that all lean toward the same hurtful assumption: "That girl is naive." Let me tell you, there is a big difference between being inexperienced and being naive. We all grow up in the same world; it's not like we don't know what's out there or haven't been exposed to the social world. Never let anyone belittle you and do not let the opinions of other people define your value. I want you to remember one thing: what you are doing—having high standards, being single, not hooking up with strangers— is not a sign that you are really still twelve years old and never grew up. It is a *choice* you have made; it is not a "default mode." When I got to college I realized that it is also the harder of the two choices. If I wanted to I could easily get dolled up, go to a big house party, and throw myself at almost any guy. Kissing, even having sex with someone, is no longer a rare or hard thing to find. What *is* rare is a woman who will say no to both. You are rare and your innocence is a gift, one that so many women have told me they would do anything to get back. So do not be ashamed; be proud and thankful that it is still yours.

The last thing you may hear a lot is: "So . . . are you going to be a nun?" And although the answer for you may be no, this question, unlike the other comments, should be taken as a compliment. "You mean, am I going to give up my life to serve others in a radical way and take Jesus Christ for my spouse? Well, no . . . But I've thought about it." Every single woman should consider this vocation before choosing marriage. Your vocation is the pathway that God has chosen specifically for you to help get you to heaven. It is the path that will help you find peace and fulfillment while on Earth, based on the specific set of talents that He has given you. In order to truly discern your vocation, you first have to consider both options and see the beauty in them. God made you; He knows where you will be happiest and most fulfilled. If you simply get married because everyone else is getting married, then you haven't really made a conscious choice. Some of the most beautiful women I have ever met are sisters or nuns. It may be the less common vocation, but if you feel called to it or are curious about it at all, please follow your heart. Research it or talk to some sisters. They are amazing women and they won't try to make you enter a religious order if that's not what God is calling you to, so there's no harm in learning more.

No matter what the future holds, for right now you are single, you are beautiful, and you are saving yourself and your body for a man who is first worthy of your heart. There is absolutely nothing to regret about that. Enjoy this time. You get the chance to make amazing girlfriends, explore new hobbies, discover which career path you may be called to, travel, learn new things about yourself and who you are, and pursue Christ. Your life doesn't begin when you find a guy. *Life is now.* Don't always be worried about finding the right person. If you first become confident in your true self, then you will know that when a man steps into your life and falls in love with you, it is the *real* you who he is loving. Let the Creator of Life and the Author of Love write your own personal love story. No story you or Disney could come up with will ever be more beautiful. Just like a father who protects his daughter from unworthy men, if you entrust your heart to God, your Father, He won't let you end up with the wrong guy—so trust in His guidance.

> A woman's heart should be so hidden in God that a man has to seek Him just to find her.—Max Lucado

Remember, anything worth having is worth waiting for. In fact, its worth only increases with time and rarity. When you do finally walk down the aisle and hear those Cinderella wedding bells ringing, you will be able to do so with your full heart and your full self. You will be able to look in the eyes of the man you love and say, "This is what I waited for. I waited for you. So that I can be yours, and only yours." In that moment, you won't feel unsure about your decision anymore.

As for my love story, it is still being written, and I can't wait to see how it plays out. God brought me a man when I least expected it and when I had given up looking. Through him I've learned that a good man, a man who truly cares about you, will not care how "inexperienced" you are or how terrified you are the first time you let him kiss you. Ladies, good men do exist! Don't lose hope. They will treat you like the princess that you are and they will treasure your innocence—helping to protect it, not tarnish it. In fact, as my boyfriend has told me before, the very fact that we carefully choose whom we date makes the men we date want to live up to our standards. As Bishop Sheen said, "To a great extent the level of any civilization is the level of its womanhood. When a man loves a woman, he has to become worthy of her." We can be women like this—women who inspire men to grow. This is the power that our love can have in this world if we let it. So what are we waiting for?

3. "How Many Guys Have I Kissed?" (Megan)

"You're such a slut." I know my friends were joking but I still feel the pain of those words to this day. The first time this was said to me was five years ago. *You think I'm a slut?* I thought, *I'll give you a slut.* If I'm being honest, that's where it all started for me—in the joking words of a friend.

You never truly know how valuable something is to you until you lose it. When it's gone it's gone forever, and only then do you see the worth you couldn't have known was there all along. So now what? Well, there are two choices you have moving forward: the realization and glorification of what was lost; or the denial that there was any worth in what you lost to begin with, in order to save yourself the pain.

What if your innocence is gone forever? What then?

At first I chose denial. I fought my conscience and filled my mind with the media's lies. I watched trashy TV shows, listened to degrading music, read *Cosmo* tips, and surrounded myself with people who supported who I was becoming and even encouraged it. I kept secrets that ate away at me. I lost the value of a kiss and turned it into a game; a night out wasn't a success unless I kissed a cute guy. I craved guys' attention and learned just how to get it. I morphed into someone I hardly recognized before I even understood what was happening. And the deeper I got into it the more I felt I had to keep it up. It was an inner battle I fought for years.

Sitting here trying to explain to you where I've been and what I've done since that day so long ago is so much more painful than I thought it would be. I fell into the ways of the world. I've been a friend with benefits, I've made out with strangers in bars, clubs, and parties, and I've been drugged, abused, and manipulated. I can't even count how many guys I've kissed—let alone tell you many of their names. Men have desired, damaged, used, forgotten, and hurt me. What's worse, I let them. I lost sight of my own value and worth and numbed myself to the emptiness within me; and when that didn't work, I drank away the pain. I learned I was worth nothing more than my body. I wanted to be wanted, but for all the wrong reasons. I felt like damaged goods.

I can't go back and change my past and I don't dwell on it. I'm not like my sweet friend you've just read about. We've taken very different paths on the way to learning about love, and I admire her determination and high standards more than I can put into words. I applaud anyone else who shares a similar story and willpower. I am not that person. I've screwed up, a lot—but I know I'm not alone.

I've made my share of mistakes in my past and I'm very blessed for the situations I've made it out of in one piece. It took me a long time to come to terms with and forgive what I had done, and what had been done to me.

By the grace of God, I met this amazing guy in the process of turning my life around. He was raised well and treated me the way a real man should. I'd never been shown that kind of respect before and I wasn't sure what to do with it. I didn't think men could be trusted anymore, so at first I ran from it. However, the more I prayed and grew closer to my faith, the more I came to learn I deserve to be treated with the dignity, kindness, and respect this man was showing me. He reminded me of my worth in Christ, and for that I am forever grateful.

I said it before and I'll say it again, be a woman who demands respect. I was not this woman for the longest time. I thought the hookup culture was what I wanted and it seemed to be the perfect match between my desire to feel wanted and a man's desire for my body. But the world deceives us when it comes to love. It teaches us to chase the boys and ditch the attachment and commitment. It tells us to just do what feels good. However, what *feels good* isn't always right and it's not always what is actually *good for us*. So wherever you are at right now in your life, take a second to stop and ask yourself what your motives are in your search for love. Are these motives leading you to act in a way that will lead you to the type of love you truly long for?

If you're single, don't lower your standards. Keep your heart rooted in God and trust that He will guide you to the right man. Don't try to force anything that isn't there because it doesn't work. I've also learned that being single is not an excuse to flirt with or kiss anyone you want. Your attention is special and shouldn't be spread to those who next month won't mean a thing to you. Focus on the people who truly matter and make you a better person. Your kisses should also be earned, because a kiss is much more valuable than we tend to realize. It's intimate and should be saved for someone you truly care about, so don't waste them.

If you're dating or in a relationship, what is your intention? Are you dating just to date, or are you discerning whether this person is someone you could marry? The end goal of dating is to find your future spouse. You're either going to get married or break up in the end, so is this someone who you could spend the rest of your life with? Does he treat you with the love and respect you deserve? Don't settle, and don't ever feel like you are stuck. Also don't be afraid to challenge aspects of your relationship. If he is a good man, he will want to change those aspects, too. If not, get out.

A solid relationship has its foundation rooted in Christ. Without God in the center we fall to selfishness and temptations. Marriage is a serious sacrament, one not taken seriously enough nowadays. God binds one man and one woman to become one flesh and create life. This means that the discernment process for marriage shouldn't be taken lightly either; it's your future marriage that is on the line. If your future husband's girlfriend was behaving or dressing as you do, would you be okay with that?

It is *so* important to set physical boundaries for yourself and stick to them. Sex is beautiful. It is the union between man and woman that creates intimacy and life. But it is meant for marriage. Sex outside of marriage is like a fish out of water—lacking the very substance that gives its existence meaning. You are not created to have such an intimate bond with others who are not your spouse, the one person who you have committed your life to. I can't tell you how far is too far, or to do *this* but not *that*. But I can tell you from experience that the further you push back that line the more difficult it will be to hit the breaks. Do yourself a favor and don't put yourself in that situation. You know when it's just kissing and when it's *kissing*. Have the courage to stop and take a step back.

Remember: women are Crock-Pots and men are toasters. We take a while to get heated up but they can turn right on. Don't let yourself get carried away in the heat of the moment. Be proactive and avoid those situations that will compromise both you and him. As much as you may desire to be the woman your man *wants*, instead, be the woman that he *needs*. Meaning that you become the woman who inspires him to be a better man, not the one who tempts him not to be. Strangely enough, he ends up wanting you more.

Also, there is an important distinction between virginity and purity. Virginity depends on whether or not scientifically speaking you have had sexual intercourse, while the definition of purity is to be morally clean and without blemish. This purity is only possible through God. In the sacrament of confession, we ask God to wipe our sins away and make us new. There is nothing that God is not capable of forgiving; all we need do is ask. He loves you and is waiting for you to return to Him.

> Anyone who belongs to Christ has become a new person. The old life is gone; a new life has begun. And all of this is a gift from God, who brought us back to Himself through Christ. And has given us this task of reconciling people to Him.—2 Corinthians 5:17–18

You don't have to be a "virgin" to be pure; purity is a way of life. Whether it was your choice to lose your virginity or it was taken from you, you can be made new. One of my favorite songs is "You Are More" by Tenth Avenue North. I listened to it so much while I struggled through forgiving myself, forgiving those who had hurt me, and making life changes.

> This is not about what you've done,
> But what's been done for you.
> This is not about where you've been,
> But where your brokenness brings you to.

Being broken is an opportunity to rebuild and to grow into a stronger woman. Our mistakes do not define us and we are so much more than the darkness of our past. Please know that if you are reading this with any past or present guilt, pain, temptations, or denial, *you don't have to feel this way.* You can make a change. It is *never* too late and there is no sin that God cannot forgive. He loves and cares for you unconditionally; all you have to do is ask. He is waiting there, arms open, for you to let Him hold you and restore you.

I can't tell my future husband that I saved my whole heart and self for him. I gave pieces of myself away to men who didn't matter along the way and that is something he and I will both have to live with in the future. However, that doesn't mean he'll love me less or that I don't deserve to be loved. It means I needed to change my ways and make things right with God. There is an anonymous quote going around that says, "Everyone comes with baggage—find someone who will help you unpack." The right man for me will be forgiving of my past, not condemning, and will be the one to help me unpack. He will still treat me the way a real man should treat a lady. We all deserve love like this, no matter where we have been; we are made for love like this.

4. NOT-SO-HAPPILY EVER AFTER

Now let's look deeper into this love that exists between *one man* and *one woman*—this inseparable divine bond that is created in marriage and that makes the two become one. Men and women are physically and emotionally complementary; each bring something new to the relationship that the other is lacking. However, many people in our world have lost their belief in the idea of monogamous love, and this has led to a diminished understanding of sex, that is, the physical aspect of the marriage union, as well as an increase in divorce. So it is time to talk about the *greatness* of sex and all that it was created to be. (We bet you didn't think that the Church loves sex, huh?)

First we will focus on the science of sex. When we have sex, a bonding hormone called oxytocin is released in our brain along with countless other hormones, such as dopamine—the pleasure hormone. Oxytocin in particular acts like a drug in our system, and in fact is often referred to as the "love drug." Oxytocin is meant to strengthen your bond with your spouse and can even help you forget the details of a petty fight. Really it is a biological gift that helps spouses stay together. Unfortunately, this same hormone is the reason it is harder to clearly see flaws in dating relationships if a couple is sexually active. As a drug, it impairs your ability to think clearly about the person you have just bonded with. Oxytocin—particularly in women, because it is released in even higher doses in women—creates an "illusion" that the person that you are with is "your perfect partner" and completely "trustworthy."[27] So if you haven't already chosen that man as your perfect partner and married him, proving his trustworthiness, then you are biologically just fooling yourself.

Oxytocin also contributes to why it hurts so much when it ends. If you are bonded to a man in every way possible—emotionally, physically, and even chemically—and have given so much of yourself to him, then it is going to hurt to leave him. This is why sex was meant only for marriage, only for the one man you have chosen to give yourself to completely with your heart first, and who has committed his life to you and only you. It is to *protect you.*

Still don't agree with this? Maybe you think that sex is an act of the body and since it is your body you should be able to do whatever you want with whomever you want. Maybe you believe that if you truly love someone, *then* it is okay; you don't need to be married. Well, if you do think any of these things we don't blame you. Why wouldn't you? That's what society is telling all of us.

However, place yourself in this scenario for a second (which was once shared with us by a friend). Picture yourself meeting the man of your dreams. He is everything you have ever wanted and then some. You plan your dream wedding, you celebrate with your friends, and then you go on a honeymoon together to a tropical paradise. You have sex, confirming with your body everything that you just said in your vows. There is nothing more beautiful that you could physically do together, and you now share absolutely everything with one another—body, heart, soul, and lives. After the honeymoon, you go back to your newly purchased apartment to begin your life together and you couldn't be happier!

One day you and your husband are outside when you see a woman, your next-door neighbor, out walking her dog. You sense that something is wrong, so you question your husband until he finally looks at you and tells you that that woman is the ex-girlfriend he'd told you about—the one he lost his virginity to before you entered his life.

Now every day that you see this woman you hardly know, you can't help but think that there is nothing you and your husband have shared physically that she has not shared with him as well. *That hurts.*

It wasn't supposed to be this way. Yes, this scenario is made up, but you have to admit that in our world today it's not impossible. It's certainly not rare that one or both of the spouses will no longer be a virgin when they get married. In a 2006–2010 survey conducted by the Center for Disease Control and Prevention, 63 percent of young women and 64 percent of young men ages 15 to 19 reported that they had premarital sex; and not many people marry by the age of 19, so that number only increases with age.[16] Between ages 19 and 44 it jumps to 86 percent of women and 90 percent of men.[16] That's practically only 1 in 10 people who are virgins when they get married.

When you're sharing you, *all of you*, with the man you love so much that you want to be with him forever, do you really want to share this level of intimacy with all of his previous ex-lovers? No. This is not how we were created. There will always be lingering questions: Am I as good as his last? Even though he loves me, does he remember her body in this way, too? These thoughts build and drive us crazy. They lead to fights and detachment to avoid the pain. This is not the plan for us. We are meant to be completely joined in love, and vulnerable without fear.

People often say, "Well, we're probably going to get married someday, so we want to live together first to test this out. There's nothing wrong with that, right?" Let's pretend that this is you asking this question, and you decide to go ahead with it. You and your boyfriend move in to the same place, the same bed, and start to get to learn about each other in a completely new, raw, and exciting way. You get to be roommates with the man you love, while getting to check if you're compatible, both sexually and in your daily lifestyle. Win-Win! This way, if you don't like his quirks or you decide you want out, you can walk away because there's no real commitment. It's like being married but without the vows.

Okay, but now think about the fact that he is asking these exact same questions about *you*. He's noticing your quirks, your lifestyle, and your physical "compatibility" with him, all the while knowing that he can get out at any moment if he sees something that he doesn't like.

Tell me again why this is a good idea? Why would you want to combine lives, bodies, and hearts with someone who may leave you at any moment, or if a difficulty comes up?

Part of the thrill of marriage is the start of a new life together. You join bank accounts and buy a place together to make it your home. You get to laugh through the honeymoon phase of learning that he snores way more loudly than he warned or always leaves the toilet seat up. You learn together how to make your incessant need for everything to be clean and his constantly leaving towels on the floor work because you *choose* to. You find that somehow you love him despite the fact that his breath smells terrible in the morning, and he loves you with your face cream and hair all a mess. You can be completely comfortable because when you said "I do" you meant *forever*. You're not playing house; you're building a life together. So you don't have to be afraid! This is the unconditional, lasting love we were created for, the love we long for.

Living together before marriage, having sex to make sure you're sexually compatible, it's not healthy for anyone. If you are woman and he is man, boom, you are compatible—I promise. Our bodies just fit together like puzzle pieces. Our bodies aren't meant to be tested out with different people to see who we like best. Statistics show that nonvirgins are much more likely than virgins to have marital issues and they have an increased likelihood of divorce.[23] That includes more adulterous behavior in the nonvirgin marriages, which makes sense. If you live your life thinking that sex is casual and that when relationships get hard or go south you just move on to the next one, then it's not a far jump to fall victim to cheating or be more prone to the idea of divorce. Habits don't end with a wedding ring. Statistics show couples who live together before marriage have a 40 percent higher chance of getting divorced.[30] That means you are almost doubling your chances of your marriage ending in divorce.

Divorce is a problem that we are seeing much too often nowadays. In our Western culture today, about 40 to 50 percent of marriages end in divorce.[11] We both come from families separated by divorce and we're sure many of you do as well. Everything we have been talking about is a big part of the reason why. The hookup and cohabitation culture doesn't act as preparation for lifelong commitment and fidelity. It offers an easy exit. Also, focusing on the physical parts of a relationship often leaves other important areas of relationships, like communication, badly neglected. You lose the chance to learn more about each other in different situations and the chance to discuss what marriage truly means to each of you. Marriage is a lifelong commitment, not just another stepping-stone in a relationship.

Some think that since divorce has become the norm in our society, that there is no point in fighting it. Wouldn't it just be easier to except it as an option? The problem is, divorce is not only breaking up marriages and tearing apart families, it's destroying our society. Our society is built on families. It is where all of our lives begin and grow, whether it's good or bad.

> Fatherhood and motherhood are themselves a particular proof of love; they make it possible to discover love's extension and original depth. But this does not take place automatically. Rather, it is a task entrusted to both husband and wife.—Pope St. John Paul II

Think about it. The two people who are supposed to be our first examples of unconditional, lasting love, and show us that that kind of love is not only possible but is what we are made for, break up. What does that often leave the children thinking? They learn that love is conditional, that love can't be trusted. They think that they weren't enough to make their parents stay together and maybe even believe that it is their fault.

If these doubts aren't properly addressed they can cause problems in children's future relationships, in school, in self-worth, and in discipline. A decade-long study performed at the University of Utah by Nicholas Wolfinger found that children of divorce, despite their desire to want to break the "cycle of divorce," are two times more likely to get a divorce if one spouse is from that background, and three times more likely if both are.[11] Why? Because they model the love that they have been taught.

What if we were to model a greater love? What is we were to model the Source of Love itself—the love of our Father. We have the opportunity to change the cycle from the start and have stronger, lasting relationships right now. If marriage is forever— and that's what you're called to—what does that mean for how you look at dating? If sex is meant to be a part of that forever, are you really satisfied with sex without the vows? Are you satisfied with sharing all of yourself with multiple men, and with your future husband doing the same with women? Do you really want to try to tackle the commitment to forever alone?

Marriage is a sacrament for a reason: we need God's grace. We need Christ's perfect example of selfless, sacrificial love. We're not perfect, our spouses won't be perfect, and life is not easy; but forever is possible when we realize that we are not alone. So whether you are in a relationship or not, reflect on this section and ask yourself these questions:

* What virtues are you going to look for in a future spouse, a father for your children, and provider for your family?
* How are you going to prepare yourself for marriage by working on some of these same virtuous traits? How can you become the best *you*?

* What is the foundation of the love between that cute old couple sitting next to one another still holding hands and smiling? How can you work toward love like that?
* What are you willing to do now to make your future marriage last?

For tips, advice, quotes, and book recommendations on more relationship topics, check out our website. Be proactive. There is some great information out there, so please use it!

PART IV
Faith

1. You Lost Me at *Hello* (Kaylin)

Two ways commonly used, with the greatest of intentions, to introduce people to the Christian faith are: the *scare tactic* and the *stuff-it-down-your-throat* approach. I've had people at my school literally stand on a stump with a sign that says "You Are Going to Hell" and scream "You are all sinners!" to every student who walks by. Call me crazy but no matter how good what you have to say may be, that probably won't get people to listen to you and it doesn't help them realize that it is a message of love you are trying to share with them. With the second approach, well-meaning Christians try to enforce the laws of the Church and the Bible on people who do not yet even have a reason why they should listen, or why they would want to. They don't have the heart or desire to because they have no clue who this "Jesus" person is that you are talking about, and they are most definitely not ready to change their lives for Him. Megan and I have experienced this approach in some of our religion classes at our private schools growing up. In classes like these you learn laws, definitions, verses, and prayers, which are all great things, but it often doesn't go any deeper than that if you aren't taught how to develop a relationship with Christ Himself.

Since neither of these ways really worked for us we are going to try a different approach. We are women, we like stories, right? Walk by any lunch table or Starbucks couch and you'll hear women sharing story after story with each other. Jesus even taught through stories, called parables, in order to relate to the crowds. Since we are only twenty-one and by no means anywhere close to theologians, stories are really all that we have. We'd like to share them with you—the parts of our lives that have led to our love for Christ and have brought us to where we are in our faith lives today. Our hope is that you will discover something new about Christ's pursuit of your own heart.

2. Surrender (Kaylin)

I was baptized Catholic as a child, raised by loving parents, and sent to great private schools. But I'm sure many of you have had some or all of these things in your own life, too. None of these aspects on their own, or even all of them put together, will ensure a strong faith. Many baptized Christians fall away from their faith. It happens all the time, because the only faith that lasts is a faith built on an encounter with Christ. I'm not talking about a big moment where the clouds part and God descends to you and reveals everything about life before your eyes. (If that happened that would be pretty sweet.) I'm talking about hearing about Jesus, seeing the result of His love in someone you meet or in something that happens, and beginning to recognize His presence in your own life, all around you. It is an encounter like this—a relationship discovered and then built over time—that I would like to share with you.

Like I said, I grew up very blessed. I had a loving family and friends, a good school, fun sports teams, two siblings to play with, and a good sense that there was a God who loved me. However, when seventh grade rolled around, my little world fell apart. My parents sat my brother, sister, and me down and told us that they were getting a divorce. My dad moved out and I slowly learned to stop waiting for the sound of the garage door opening at the time when he would usually get home from work.

I learned to live out of an overnight bag, and to have two rooms and two schedules. I'm sure many of you can relate to this.

As the oldest child, I felt a need to be strong. I acted excited about the new condo my Dad got and encouraged my younger siblings, telling them that everything was going to be fine. I wanted to be tough for my parents because I could tell they were hurting, too. It was hard, but I was stubborn and I wanted to regain some control, which included not allowing myself to cry.

Two short months later, I watched silently as my world changed yet again. I came home from school to find my mom lying on the kitchen floor in tears, after a phone call that confirmed she had stage 3 breast cancer, and it was growing fast. Apparently, my mom all of a sudden had a fifty-fifty chance of survival. Over the next year, she lost her hair, had countless surgeries that left her body mutilated, and had many brushes with death. The woman I loved most, a woman who was strong, physically and spiritually, who in my eyes had done everything right, was suffering more than I had ever known possible. One moment in particular that I remember was coming home to find white sheets covering every mirror in the house. My mom had just lost all of her hair and had her double mastectomy; she didn't recognize herself anymore and didn't want to try. As a seventh grade girl watching this, it was hard.

After months of moments like this, and watching her be sick in bed or wince in pain, my stubborn "I got this" approach wasn't working so well. I'd had enough. I remember running into my new room at my Dad's condo and leaning against our bunk beds, lights still off so that I was truly alone, and then finally letting the tears come. Anyone who has tried holding back tears for a long time knows that when they finally do come, they *come*. So there I am, sobbing, in the dark, alone. Out of desperation I finally turned to God. I began praying, but my prayer consisted more of me yelling at God. *Why did you do this?! Why her? She loves you so much! How could you let this happen? Why is there nothing that I can do to help her? What if she dies?* I didn't hold back; I finally let myself feel all the doubts, fears, and sorrow that I had been harboring inside. God just took it. He let me pour out all my anger onto Him and when I finally had cried my eyes out, I felt His response. An overwhelming sense of peace ran through me for the first time in months. All I could think was that I wasn't alone. I didn't have to be "strong enough," because my mom wasn't in my hands; she was in the hands of someone who loved her even more than I did. Someone who cried with her every tear, and saw her every scar. So I concluded my prayer saying, *Alright, God, I'm out of options . . . I surrender my mom to you.*

After this moment, I was able to see the whole experience from a new perspective. Knowing that the future was out of my control somehow released me to live in the present. I began to focus on the moments that I did have with my mom, whether there would be five more months of them or fifty years (even though I was praying hard for the latter). By doing this I started to realize that yes, my mom was suffering, but she was somehow still happy. She never stopped singing, never stopped dancing, never stopped making jokes about the looks she got for her bald head, and she also never stopped thanking God for each new day of life. If she could see the blessings in life, how could I not learn to do the same? I saw joy in her and knew that it was not her own. How could it be? She had seemingly nothing to be joyful about! She was fighting for her life while going through a divorce—not exactly an ideal combination. It had to be God.

So I took the lessons I learned through these times to high school with me. I felt so blessed to have learned what is truly important in life and the effects that gratitude can have on a situation. My mom recovered and her hair grew back in, and both of my parents, after the pain of the divorce and after receiving an annulment, got remarried—to two people that I can't imagine my life without now. Everything seemed to be calming down again; but we all know that life doesn't work like that, it tends to mix things up every once and a while.

During my junior year of school I got the chance to test what I had learned with my mom on myself. I began getting frequent migraines, culminating with nine in one month. I'm sure that many of you have experienced at least one migraine in one of the many forms they can come in. For me, a "migraine" meant losing half of my vision and curling up in my bed for about six hours, as it felt like a machine was not only stabbing my head on every side but also compressing it until I was sure that it would implode. Sometimes it would make me get sick to my stomach, or the left side of my face and arm would go numb, but luckily those were more rare. No matter what, when my vision began to fail I would drop what I was doing and find a way to get home before the real pain started up. Then I would cry in helplessness as I waited the six hours out. No amount of Advil or Excedrin helped; there was nothing I could do.

I began to live in fear. I never knew when one would come, or what I'd be doing or whom I'd be with when it did. When the vision-block came, I knew that no matter what I did intense pain was on its way. I had my eyes tested, had an MRI done for tumors, and tracked what foods I ate to look for triggers, but we found nothing. There were no answers. The doctors finally concluded that it was hormonal; aka, there was nothing concrete that I could do. Before I knew it, I had lost the lessons I'd learned early in life. I went back to feeling *I am alone.* I couldn't even depend on my own body not to hurt me anymore. I couldn't even think about something else to take my mind off of it because it felt like it was my mind that was malfunctioning.

Thankfully, since I had forgotten for myself, God used my mom and family and friends to remind me that I wasn't alone and I wasn't helpless. Through them, I found Him again. I let Him into those moments of fear, pain, and sorrow, and sure enough, He once again began to transform them. Suddenly I wasn't alone crying, I was in His arms crying. The whole notion of gratitude also came back into my life, and I became so incredibly thankful for each day that I was healthy, each day that I could look around and see everything clearly. We often take our health for granted, but it doesn't take much to realize what a mistake that is. I also realized that in my own moments of pain and suffering I was better able to relate to other people suffering from far worse things than me. This connection acted as a reminder for me to pray for them. Eventually I found a medicine that shortened the duration of the episodes and dulled the pain, which made my migraines much more bearable.

This time in my life reminded me of the lesson I had learned early on: *I am not strong enough to handle this life on my own.*

No matter how stubborn I was, I finally had to realize that this lesson wasn't going to be a one-time thing. It was going to be a daily thing—a *daily surrendering*. I listened to this song a lot during this time, as a reminder of this:

> When I'm finally
> Finally at rock bottom,
> Well, that's when I start looking up
> and reaching out . . .
> I know I'm not strong enough to be
> Everything that I'm supposed to be,
> I give up
> I'm not strong enough.
> Hands of mercy, won't you cover me
> Lord right now I'm asking you to be
> Strong enough,
> Strong enough, for the both of us.
> —Matthew West, "Strong Enough"

No matter what, everyone suffers in some way as a result of our fallen world. What I've learned is that we can either succumb to self-pity and live in fear, letting our suffering define us, *or* we can surrender it to Christ and watch, as my mom used to say, as "the rose unfold from the thorns." Through my life I have realized that surrendering myself to Christ means giving Him what I can't handle and admitting to Him that I am not strong enough. Most important, it means surrendering to my Father and Creator's loving plan for me, and knowing that I am never alone.

Jesus Christ himself was: tempted by the devil, went without food for forty days in the desert, betrayed by one of his best friends, captured and unjustly condemned, spat at and mocked by those who had loved him, abandoned in His time of need, whipped and tortured, forced to carry a heavy cross up a hill, nailed to that cross, and killed. There is nothing that we can suffer, big or small, that He did not also suffer. He did all of this because of His love for each of us, and His great desire to resurrect that love and life from the very depths of our suffering.

We have to realize that *God does not cause suffering.* Do you think that He would cause His own Son to be treated like this, or His beloved daughter and the mother of three kids to have cancer? No. However, God can work through this suffering, through the brokenness of our fallen world, to bring about a greater good. He longs to do this for us but we have to let Him. Out of love He has given us *free will,* so now we must choose to let Him be a part of our lives, and not only a part of our greatest burdens, but our smaller daily ones as well. By inviting Christ into those moments of insecurity, fear, loneliness, or anxiety, we can ask Him to help us trust in His amazing ability to make good come from nothing. He always has a plan to restore us from our state of brokenness. These are His words for us:

Lay down your burdens,
Lay down your shame.
All who are broken,
Lift up your face.
Oh wanderer come home
You're not too far.

So lay down your hurt,
Lay down your heart,
Come as you are.—David Crowder, "Come As You Are"

We can't choose what happens to us in this life, but we *can* choose how we respond. I invite you to surrender whatever you are going through to Christ. Then watch as He takes it and molds it into something so much more than you ever could have imagined possible.

3. Joyful Trust (Megan)

We are all united in this experience of suffering. Maybe we've watched friends and family suffer, maybe we've suffered ourselves, or maybe we've seen strangers in times of suffering. The key is that we must not lose hope in these times. Like my friend beautifully said with her story, we have the opportunity to surrender our struggles, our lives, our hopes and dreams, and everything that we are to God. So if we choose to make that leap of faith, then what? What do we do while we wait for God to make something of our feeble offering of self?

We trust.

I will be the first to tell you that I had trust issues. Key word: had. Okay, let's be honest, sometimes it's *have*. Trust is a big deal. It's difficult to gain and oh so easy to lose. Like my friend, I was born and raised in a loving, supportive Catholic family. I have the most caring parents in the world, two half sisters I whole love (anyone with half siblings should get that), and the best big brother I could ever want—but I was a stress on my family very early in life. Just before the age of three I was diagnosed with acute lymphocytic leukemia. This is a form of cancer that basically means that my white blood cells weren't functioning properly, and since it was acute, it was fast acting. I was hospitalized immediately after the diagnosis and spent weeks fighting for my short life.

Like the book *The Fault in Our Stars* said, "The only thing worse than biting it from cancer, is having a kid bite it from cancer."[6] I can't even imagine the stress and pain it put my family through. I still see the agony in their faces any time my cancer is brought up. That time during my treatment, though, was where I first saw the power of trust in God.

My mom was raised Lutheran and converted to the Catholic faith when she married my dad. She had a strong belief in God, but to her He was a distant God. It took her finding out that her youngest daughter might not survive for that to change. Then it became real; God became real. She surrendered everything she had to faith and put her whole trust in God. It wasn't until I was older that I truly realized what this must have taken for her to do. My mother's example, her ability to surrender the life of her child into His loving hands, showed me God's ability to work miracles and taught me how important it is to place my trust in Him—*no matter what.*

The first time this trust in God was put to the test for me was when my parents decided to get a divorce. It was the end of my third-grade year and at the young age of nine I had no idea what that meant—only that it was bad. In the next few years my family completely split in two. I was left in the middle, all alone, fighting for what scraps were left of what I had known to be family. If you can imagine the most horrible, nasty divorce—that was what my family went through. When I say I was alone, I mean I was the only person on either side who could talk to anyone in the family without fighting, prejudice, or dislike. I love my family, every last crazy one of them, but we were broken.

So I did the only thing my little nine-year-old self really could do in this situation: I *prayed*. I prayed every single day that God would reunite us and somehow make us whole again. My hope carried on until one day in middle school, I finally gave up. I had been praying for over five years without an answer and I was tired, hurt, torn, and still alone. I told God I was done, because He obviously wasn't going to do anything to heal us.

Later that same day I walked into my mom's house and saw my brother hanging up the phone. He told me he had called our dad for the first time in years and that they were going to get lunch. I stood there, my mouth gaping open in shock. He acted like it was the most casual thing, not knowing that in that simple moment my hope was renewed and my prayers had finally been answered.

The thing is, as the *Catechism of the Catholic Church* says, "whether or not our prayer is heard depends not on the number of words but on the fervor of our hearts."[19] God knew the right time to answer my prayers. He may not have answered me when I wanted, but he did answer my call. He felt my pain and He loved me through it; and for that I will forever be grateful. From this experience I learned that God does hear us and He does care, but we must learn to trust in His timing. Sometimes the answer is *no*, or *wait*, or *I have something better in store*, but God will never leave our prayers unanswered. Love is not always what you want to hear, but it is always what you need to hear. If He's asking you do something, it's because He knows something you don't—or maybe that you do but don't want to admit to.

I like having things all figured out and having a schedule and a back-up plan. The thing is, my plan normally doesn't match up with what God has in store for me. But I know now that if we're open to God's plan and timing, He has some pretty incredible things in store for us. All we have to do is trust in Him.

I've learned, as you saw earlier, that God loves me *as I am*. I never needed to starve, overexert, or make myself sick to be beautiful. I never had to search for love in all the wrong places, only to wind up in so much pain, and I didn't need to turn to drinking to numb the ache. But I do not regret these moments of my life because all this hurt and these mistakes brought me to where I am today—they brought me to my God's loving arms. This is where I am loved. This is where I am safe. Despite every mistake I continue to make, I have my God to fall back on. And that, my friends, is why I depend on my faith life and community so much. I am not alone and I do not have to have it all planned out. I just have to *surrender* and *trust*.

There have been many times in my life when I've felt alone and lost, as I'm sure you've felt, too. In those moments I have had to relearn, to a greater depth, the truth of these two powerful words. My second-to-last semester of college I had the opportunity to study abroad in beautiful Florence, Italy. It was the experience of a lifetime and I couldn't be more grateful for the mistakes and fumblings that led me to it. I was able to travel and grow in so many exciting new ways. I learned more about language and culture than I ever thought possible; but I was also going through more agony than I could've ever imagined. The first man I had ever been brave enough to love broke up with me just hours before I got on the plane, and I didn't know a single person I was studying abroad with. I had no one to turn to. I felt alone and I cried for days, until I finally reached a point where God helped open my eyes to see that even at my lowest points I had never really been alone.

This pivotal moment occurred when a priest came to visit our campus and offer Mass. Beforehand he gave us the chance to go to confession and I opted to go immediately, as I had so many times before. Confession is one of the most beautiful sacraments and one of my personal favorites. Christ himself wipes away our tears and sins and offers us healing from our past mistakes and comforting words through the priest. This priest in particular offered me advice that has completely changed my perspective on life. He told me to not only trust in God, but to *daily choose joy*. I had never really thought of joy as a choice before—or as a product of surrendering my suffering.

Even in the most difficult times we can choose to be happy because our joy is not within ourselves, but in our Savior, Jesus Christ. I began to slowly give every broken piece of my heart to God, every day, to mend. It was the hardest thing I have ever done but it was in that pain that I found healing and life like never before. I pray that you experience this joyful freedom and healing in your own lives as well.

I have learned that I need to stop asking where God is in a situation; He is always there with me. Instead, I need to ask Him to reveal Himself to me, and He will. When I did this I realized that He was there, comforting me, I just hadn't looked up to see Him. I forgot to trust as I had earlier in my life.

Now whenever I feel alone, I remind myself that I am His. Whenever I am lost, I trust that He is holding on to me. Whenever I feel unworthy, I remind my heart that I am worth *dying* for. Every day I wake up and I choose joy. I notice that on the days I forget to choose joy nothing seems to go right. However, I can turn my day around by simply redirecting my thoughts and attitude. My joy is not of this world. It is not a fleeting happiness. It is built firmly on my faith and trust in God, and my hope in all that He does for me.

I'm currently embarking on the scariest journey college has to offer: *graduation*. I don't know what's ahead or where I am going or what to do next; but I am able to confidently move forward into the unknown because I know that I am not alone. I know that God has a plan even when I don't.

There isn't enough room in your mind for both worry and faith. You must decide which one will live there.
—Anonymous Pinterest quote

God asks us to have a childlike faith in Him. Jesus said, "Let the little children come to me, and do not hinder them, for the kingdom of God belongs to such as these. Truly I tell you, anyone who will not receive the kingdom of God like a little child will never enter it" (Mark 10:14–15). Children are naturally humble and teachable, and they trust their parents to lead them where they need to go. In that same way, we are called to be God's children and trust in His plan. He knows what will make us truly happy and our joy is found in coming to know His deep love for us. Ask yourself these questions about your own journey moving forward:

* Are you ready for Christ to take the lead in your life?
* Do you trust that He will guide you to what will truly make you happy?
* Have you experienced the joy that surrendering can bring?
* Are you willing to give it a shot?

4. Give Faith a Try

We can't just tell you to "have faith," because as we said in the beginning of Part IV, that doesn't work. All we can do is share with you what a difference faith has made in our lives and hope that you choose to embrace faith on your own. No matter where you are at in your life right now, God will meet you there. God is a person. So if He's a stranger to you, start the same way you would with any other person: introduce yourself to Him. Learn about Him and slowly let Him learn about you. Yes, He knows everything about you already (He did create you), but He *wants* to hear it from you.

If God is already your best friend, then look at the places in your heart that you are keeping Him out of and let Him in. Grow more with Him and in Him, and begin to invite Him into your life experiences in new ways. Continue to seek His heart and choose to allow Him to pursue yours. Then help introduce Him to those who are lost around you.

Dive deeper into your faith through Scripture, new forms of prayer, faith-filled relationships with others, and by learning more about the Church's teachings. There are a million ways to get closer to God, so just start somewhere. (Visit our website for resources to help you do this.) The Church and the community within it are here to help you, not hinder you.

One thing that always helps us in both our lives is to remember this quote:

Keep your eyes always on the Son, and the shadows will fall behind you.—Adapted from a Walt Whitman quote

PART V

Twenty-first-Century Buzz Topics

1. "You Do You"

IN OUR SOCIETY TODAY, MANY have forgotten what it means for something to be *true*. A quick Google dictionary search says that in order for something to be true it has to be "consistent with fact or reality, real, genuine"; something that is "without variation" and "unswerving."[25] So why is it that when people start asking the harder questions, like "Is it wrong to kill?" "Is there a God?" and so on, people are quick to say, "Well, it *depends* on the person, it *depends* on the culture, it *depends* on their truths"? Based on its definition, truth does not depend on varying circumstances.

Let's take a look at what may be going on here by looking at different aspects of truth.

A. TRUTH EXISTS

We both love to travel! We love to experience different cultures, lifestyles, and people around the world. Every city we go to has its own unique and exciting style. One of the greatest lessons we have learned through traveling is that it is in the *diversity* of life that its *universality* emerges.

Our world is vast, diverse, and beautiful. Each person is completely distinctive; and yet no matter what language people may speak, or what amount of money they may have, or whether they live in a mansion or a mud hut, *humanity is humanity*. There is a likeness to us all. That's why we can communicate without words. A smile means the same thing here as it does in Thailand, "the Land of Smiles." The cry of a baby is the same across cultures. An act of love, or a kind gesture, is appreciated in the same way everywhere.

So yes, we may each be different and one of a kind, but that doesn't mean there are not certain things that remain *true*—always. Let's take, for example, the laws of physics, which are considered by all to be accepted truths. No scientist created them, but all scientists can recognize that they are observable facts and part of creation, just as we are. For a more visual example, if we brought you a monkey, regardless of what word your culture may have for it or the connotations you may associate with it, the monkey itself does not change.

Truth does exist.

B. SCIENCE AND RELIGION *ARE* CONNECTED

There is a natural order in our world. It is not an order that we created but it is an order that we can certainly observe, as we observe physical laws and identities. No human can make gravity turn off or the Earth stop spinning. So how did it get like this?

One of the laws of physics is the law of conservation of matter. The dictionary describes this as "a fundamental principle of classical physics that matter cannot be created or destroyed in an isolated system."[25] Basically, that means that *something* cannot come from *nothing*. Where *can* it come from? It can be transferred into a new system from an already existing system. So where did the universe, the Earth, and humanity come from? From an existing source: our Creator, God. Whether or not you believe in things like the Big Bang theory or multiverses, something or someone had to start it all.

To say that science and religion, fact and heart, the physical and the spiritual, are not connected would be like saying our physical bodies have nothing to do with who we are internally. Our physical world and spiritual world are very much intertwined, and humanity is the culmination of this connection.

True science discovers God in an ever-increasing degree—as though God were waiting behind every door. —Pope Pius XII

The impossibility of conceiving that this grand and wondrous universe, with our conscious selves, arose through chance, seems to me the chief argument for the existence of God.—Charles Darwin

Science asks questions, traces facts, gives words to observations, and tries to discover meaning. God's role in this search is that He is the Maker of all that science is observing. He created the order of our universe which, if left to itself, would naturally descend into chaos, yet instead is very much governed by laws. God is all that is left when a scientist reaches the end of a trail; we must conclude that some things are beyond us, beyond our understanding, and beyond our capabilities. God is the infinite mystery that fuels the unending search. The mystery in this physical world is merely an image of all that is to be discovered within Him.

C. True Joy

Let's take a different approach to what *truth* is. Picture an ordinary scene of a mother with her children at the park. One child sees something new and exciting and quickly says, "Mommy, mommy, what's that?" Imagine that the mother looks at her child and says, "Well, it depends on who you ask, honey."

What child would be satisfied with that answer? That's not exactly what we are looking for when we ask a question, and the same holds true as we get older. *Who am I? What is my purpose? What is the meaning of life?* We can't help but wonder these things, especially during pivotal moments in our lives when we are being confronted with decisions regarding the future. However, we are being answered in the same way that this child was. The world has hundreds of answers to these questions, which leaves us thinking that we have to choose the answer for ourselves, any answer. How are we, with about twenty years of life experience, supposed to do this? We were created for a reason, we know this in our hearts, but as creations we can't look to ourselves to find the answers. We must look to our Creator.

We can do this by looking at clues He has given us in the universal aspects of humanity. For example, let's consider what drives our lives and motivates us. What do a serial killer, a meth addict, a CEO, a professional athlete, an alcoholic, a priest, and a college student all have in common? They are all seeking *happiness*. In each of these examples the factor producing the person's happiness is drastically different, but ultimately that same force is driving them all. This desire for happiness in our lives was meant to lead us to the very source of happiness. Not happiness as in the happiness of devouring a chocolate sundae, but a much deeper and lasting happiness that we could call *joy*. This is the one *true* version of happiness.

Just like with beauty in the first part of the book, this desire for happiness is meant to lead us back to our Creator. Only He, who created us and knows us better than we know ourselves, knows where we will each find this joy. Only a love that is unconditional, a truth that is undebatable, and a joy that is unquenchable will fulfill us. He knows this, and He also knows that shiny objects easily distract us. That's precisely why He instilled this desire within us, so that we would be left wanting and we would keep searching until we find lasting joy—in Him. Most of the things in life that make us happy aren't bad, but they are fleeting. If we place too much of ourselves in things that provide temporary fulfillment, we will never be fully satisfied. We get the newest iPhone, the latest fashion trend, the flashiest car, the best-paying job . . . Now what? There has to be more.

What happens if our drugs, alcohol, parties, money, favorite food, car, health, clothes, or friends are taken from us? Then only the joy that does not come from this world, a joy that resides in our hearts and that no one can take, will remain. This kind of joy comes from a place of knowing that we are not alone, that our lives matter, and that we are made for a life beyond this physical world. It comes from our Creator who made us for that life beyond this world. It is a joy strong enough to accompany martyrs to their deaths and to instill them with peace when they have been stripped of all else. That is the depth of this kind of joy.

To help us go about finding this invisible joy in our physical world, God has given us the Church. The Church is His gift to us to help guide us. She is a good mother with true answers for us, her children, about the life we have been given. As any mother should, the Church wants nothing more than for all of her children to find the love of the Father and deep joy in their lives. Her thousands of years of tradition and history give her *thousands* of years of wisdom and the answers to the very same questions that we are asking today—because they are the same ones that have been asked for centuries.

When a mother tells her child not to touch fire, the child has two options: listen and avoid being burned, or disobey and get burned. Either way, the child learns that the mother was telling the *truth*. The mother's hope, of course, is that the child trusts in her love for him or her enough to listen, but if not, she will comfort and help heal the child after he or she is burned.

Each of us has been that child, the one touching the fire to see if it is indeed dangerous; but we don't have to keep getting burned. We can choose to trust, to let ourselves be guided away from danger and toward a greater joy. So now we ask you to challenge yourself and ask yourself these questions:

- What makes you happy? Have you ever been left wanting?
- Are you satisfied with the truths you've been told, or truths that you have adopted? Are you still searching for real answers?

* In all the ways that you are searching, are you willing to include Christ as a possible answer? What do you have to lose?
* What if there really is a God? A God who created you and wants to love you, restore you, and fill you with joy? A God who longs to give you truthful answers to your questions and direction to your life? Is a God like this worth the search?

You are made to want to know the truth. Never let anyone tell you that there is no truth, because the very definition of the word makes that impossible. Believing that "there is *no truth*" is in itself a statement that many are trying to make *a truth* for everyone. So ask questions, stay curious, and seek truth at its Source. It just may unlock the answers you've been looking for. Never be afraid to ask questions, because truth won't change the more you question it—that's the point of truth, it's unwavering. However, you do have to seek it to find it.

Now do this with the sections you are about to read. Open your mind, do some research, and don't be afraid of the truth, of something that may challenge what you believe. Go ahead, challenge it right back and find the facts for yourself. Go to your local church and question a priest, e-mail and question us, or do anything else you want; the only thing that we don't want you to do is *nothing*. Don't shut off or become indifferent because this stuff really does matter; it's a big part of the world you live in and is affecting your life.

2. "DRINK TO GET DRUNK" (MEGAN)

It is impossible in our generation to make it out of high school and college without at least being exposed to the first topic we want to cover: alcohol and drugs. The peer pressure to join in on the fun is unreal. Those who are strong enough to resist are mocked for it, while those who fall to the temptations of fitting in often feel trapped.

I'm sure you've heard it before, but *alcohol kills more teenagers than all other drugs combined* and is a factor in the three leading causes of death among fifteen to twenty-four-year-olds: accidents, homicides, and suicides.[4] We could go on and on with the statistics that illustrate why alcohol, and drugs in general, are wrong and harmful, but it won't make a difference. You have to decide for yourself if it's worth it. We've all heard the lectures about drinking responsibly. We've been given the pamphlets on the effects of alcohol and we've seen the pictures of what drugs do to our bodies, but it's still just an abstract idea. The consequences seem distant and avoidable as long as you are smart. When we're told, "Don't do meth," we think, "Well, yeah, of course I don't want to look like those horribly frightening pictures." Or, "Don't be an alcoholic or you're going to destroy your liver and brain function," we roll our eyes and think, "Okay, I have no intention of doing that, I just want to have some drinks with friends." Being "responsible" has lost its real meaning and instead just means "not getting caught."

"Drink to get drunk." That's a typical motto of anyone our age. We've seen it or we've experienced it ourselves. I know I did. I thought that for alcohol to be worth my time I had to

get drunk, that was the point. You needed to feel a buzz, get a little louder, and let loose. I thought it was fun and I fell into the party scene in college, wanting to fit in and forget the stress of life for a while.

College meant finally being able to shake off the high school version of myself and become whoever I wanted to be. It was a freeing feeling and I spent most of my first semester going out and drinking to get drunk like my friends; but in the back of my mind it always felt wrong. I had very little experience with alcohol before college but I didn't let anyone know that. Instead I pretended I was a pro, even though I didn't know my limits. I hated the "I know what you did last night" looks of judgment in the cafeteria the next day, but I loved the stories that I got to share with my friends and the laughs about how stupid everyone acted the night before. It got to the point where a weekend night without drinking felt like a waste.

Alcohol, like any drug, comes with a price. You give up your ability to make choices or think clearly, and you give up your free will, all for those precious drunken hours. It's just a distraction, though; when the hangover headache sets in and the morning comes, everything you were trying to escape is still waiting there for you. It's no way to cope; it's merely a diversion from real life and what actually matters.

There are nights I don't remember, nights I wish I could forget, things I've said and done that I can't take back, and all because I exchanged my ability to decide for myself for alcohol. Looking back now, as a senior in college, I see that it was a temporary fix to life, and it was me trying to fit in with people who never truly mattered and clinging to friendships that disappeared the moment I decided not to party or get drunk anymore. However, after they were gone I realized that I was so much better off without their influences in my life. I have much more sober fun with meaningful friends than I ever did with party buddies on the weekends. Alcohol is definitely good in moderation, but it's when that moderation is forgotten, as it so often is, that it becomes a huge problem. While I love going out for drinks and dancing with friends or having wine nights with my best girlfriends, I know I never want to cross the line again into letting go of my self control.

I'll be one of the first to admit that drinking is fun, but what is it costing you? Don't wait until it's too late to decide that it isn't worth it. Know your limits and know yourself well enough not to fall to pressure from others. You're worth so much more than that, even if you're not ready to believe that yet. Choose friends who will help remind you of that and who truly care about you. Seek experiences that build you up and are fun, but that don't compromise your dignity or place you in dangerous circumstances. Switching friend groups is one of the hardest things you can do, but picking the right people to surround yourself with will be one of the most important decisions you make in college. Choose carefully.

3. Contraception

We can't tell you how many times we've been to the doctor and been told to go on the pill. Oh, you have acne? The pill can help that. Bad cramps? Let's just put you on the pill to make that pain go away. Migraines? Take the pill! People nowadays act like birth control pills are some sort of miracle drug that can solve a woman's every problem. However, these pills don't actually solve anything, they only cover up the problems and can end up doing more harm than good by messing with a woman's natural hormonal system.

Some of the many possible side effects of contraceptive pills are: nausea, headaches, weight gain or loss, infertility or difficulty becoming pregnant when off the pills, altered menstrual cycle, blood clots, increased blood pressure, breast tenderness, spotting between periods, and hormonal changes.[3] An EMT once told us that he was trained to ask a young woman suffering from signs of heart failure or blood clots, "Are you on the pill?" right after "Do you smoke?" This means that EMTs are medically *trained* to know that this could be the cause of serious health effects. If you use a more invasive form of birth control, you can even cause ruptures in your uterine lining. So then why are so many women still using contraception? It's for the same reason that we get on any medication with negative side effects: the thought that "it won't happen to me." We guarantee that each of those women in the ambulance, or the ones being told that they are infertile when they are ready to have children, thought the same thing.

There is an endless list of options to chose from when it comes to contraceptives, including condoms, spermicide, patches, pills, implants, or medical procedures. No matter what a woman chooses, she is choosing either to alter her body or to block the life-giving aspects of sex in some way. This leaves room not only for physical damage to her, but for *lust* to take the place of *love* in her relationships.

Abstinence is the only form of "birth control" that is 100 percent effective and has zero side effects. You may have heard this before, but it's still not exactly the easy or popular choice these days; we know. But the thing is, our bodies are naturally designed for it. They were *designed* to create life. We as women can carry a little human being inside our wombs for months as our bodies nurture the baby's growth. How cool is that?! This is definitely something to look forward to, but in high school and college it is not something we are ready to take responsibility for. So it's as simple as this: if you are not ready for babies, you are not ready for sex. The world will tell you that if you play it smart and use your contraceptive the right way then you can have as much sex as you want, no matter what your age. However, if the condom breaks, you forget to take your pill, or Mother Nature beats out science, it's *hello baby*! And hello to a whole new level of responsibility not meant for this stage in life and not meant for you to have to do alone.

Don't put yourself in this situation, and choose instead to wait, even when it's hard, for the right timing. If you have ever been in a relationship you know how hard this can be and that's why you have to plan ahead. Set boundaries, and remember that your future husband, your future children, and your own dignity as a woman are all worth it.

So what about once you are married? What if you truly cannot have more children at a certain point in your life because of serious economic, psychological, or physical reasons? Well, it seems that God thought of that. A woman's body is not fertile 24/7. There are times in her natural cycle when fertilization can't occur, and Natural Family Planning and Fertility Awareness teach women to track that. It doesn't involve drugs or medical procedures; it is just you and your doctor tracking your personal menstrual cycle to better understand how your body works and when you are most likely to get pregnant. Then you know when to abstain from sex and when not to.

Wait, isn't that the same thing as the pill or any other form of contraception? Why can't we just use that? It's easier, and either way you're still ultimately preventing life.

There is a fundamental difference between NFP and any other form of contraception. In NFP, you never alter the woman's body or do anything to change sex as a gift of total and complete self—including your reproductive system. In any form of contraception, you do something to close that system or alter the woman's body—even though it may cause her harm. When a married couple practices NFP they express their love for one another by fully respecting every beautiful aspect of the wife's body. They work with her natural fertility cycle instead of against it, and instead of treating it as an inconvenience, they get to view it as the complex and beautiful mystery that it is. Also, NFP has the same success rate as the contraceptive pill when used correctly—over 99 percent.[17]

When you get married, you promise in your vows to be open to life and to creating a family. So whether you are practicing NFP or not, if you get pregnant you accept the child as a gift and something that you've already said yes to. Using contraceptives cannot only lead to lust instead of love within a marriage, but also to a greater disappointment with unplanned pregnancies because you were taking measures to deny that aspect of sex.

Sex is beautiful, bonding, and life-giving; but the world doesn't seem to see it in this way anymore. Contraceptives may seem like an easy "solution" to the responsibilities of sex, or whatever other problem your doctor says it can fix, but doing anything to alter your body in such a drastic way and to deny that aspect of your femininity can lead not only to physical harm but emotional harm. The so-called "responsibilities" of sex are for your protection. As we talked about in the relationship section, sex and marriage are never supposed to be separated, because giving yourself completely to a man who can leave you can lead to a broken heart and to distortion of the oneness between one man and one woman that we are made for in marriage. The gift of children is one of those "responsibilities" that help remind a husband and wife that their love is supposed to be selfless and life-giving. God uses life to protect love and to spread love.

Someday, if you are called to marriage and motherhood, you will have the privilege of carrying the child of the man you love and of bringing a new life into this world. That is an incredible and beautiful part of being a woman. So wait for that, and don't compromise your dignity as a woman by altering your body along the way. Love your body, every single aspect of it, and that will teach the man you marry one day to do the same.

4. Masturbation Myth (Kaylin)

One of the most isolating sins in our world today is masturbation. It draws you in and gives you the pleasure of being loved, teaches you to direct love toward yourself, and then leaves you—feeling more isolated than ever before and yet longing for more in order to continue to fill the emptiness.

Masturbation takes the pleasure of love while stripping love of the very depths of its original meaning. Love is meant to be a selfless gift of one person to another, but masturbation is a self-ish taking of the mere shell of love without giving anything in return.

The hurtful myth that accompanies most conversations about this topic is that it is a man's sin. It is believed that only men struggle with pornography and only men struggle with mas-turbation. This is finally changing as more women step into the light, but in the wake of this myth, a woman is left feeling com-pletely isolated if she finds herself trapped by these addictions.

If you are a woman in this situation and hearing this myth, you immediately feel as if you are the only woman in the world who is having lustful temptations in these ways. You feel dirty and ashamed of yourself for falling into the same sins time and time again. This isolation only drives you deeper into the sin, because the more you come to believe that you are unworthy of love because of what you have done, the more you desperately cling to the little bit of love that you do have—as distorted as that love may be.

The draw for a woman to fall to these temptations comes not merely from a physical origin, but from a much deeper place—a place of yearning to be wanted and loved. Yes, as women we are attracted to men; however, a man removing his shirt doesn't have quite the same effect on a woman as a woman removing her shirt does on a man. Our brains are wired differently and the devil knows this. The devil may use the physical beauty of a woman to draw a man into these actions, but he uses the longing to feel wanted and desired by a man to draw a woman in. He twists this yearning and whispers lies into her mind that justify the actions. He wants her to believe that the action is harmless and natural—even though he knows full well that he is drawing her into an unnatural form of love in order to keep pulling her further and further away from realizing the depth of the real thing.

These sins are not harmless, because they harm whomever they entrap. They rob that woman of her ability to freely love and to be pure of heart in her desire to be loved. They twist her view of her own body and turn it into an object to use as she pleases, instead of a temple that has been made to be loved, cherished, and sacred. Worst of all, these isolating sins also keep her from fully accepting the love of Christ.

The reason that I am able to speak all too well of the emotions associated with these temptations is because I struggled with masturbation myself at the end of middle school and the beginning of high school. It took a couple of years before I even realized the destructiveness of the sin I was entrapped in and ultimately was able—through the grace of God and a deeper understanding of the love I was actually looking for—to walk away from it one day. However, walking away did not allow me to leave behind the shame that had always accompanied it for me. It remained a secret, gaping wound on my heart that would resurface each time I entered the confessional, no matter how hard I tried to bury it deep inside of me and forget about it. My pride and my fear of even saying the word kept me from ever confessing it and allowing Christ to heal me. Instead I continued to live in the pain of what I had done.

Midway through my freshman year of college I had finally had enough—enough of the hidden pain and feelings of unworthiness and disgrace. So I swallowed my pride, said a few prayers, and marched myself into the confessional and for the first time in my life said the word "masturbation" out loud. Then I sat, there terrified of what the priest would say next. To my surprise, he thanked me! He thanked me, welcomed me back home, and commended me for having the courage to finally return to the arms of Christ. He told me that while sins against human love are of course wrong, they are nothing compared to the sin of pride that had kept me from receiving Christ's mercy and healing for all these years.

I was shocked. All this time I had been worried and ashamed over a sin that didn't matter at all to Christ compared to the fact that I was pushing Him away and remaining alone in my brokenness. All He wanted to do was hold me, restore me, and make me new, and I had been denying myself that freedom.

I walked out of the confessional that day feeling as if I weighed nothing at all, while tears of relief and deep healing washed down my face. It was finally over. I felt that I had been made new and realized that I had never been beyond repair—I had merely isolated myself from the One seeking to repair me. This moment embodied the very culmination of freedom for me and it is this moment that I pray happens for each and every one of you who suffer with masturbation or pornography. Do not believe the lies that you are dirty and broken. Turn to Christ who wishes to restore the true depths of love back into your life; allow yourself to be restored by His longing to love you.

Also, know that you are not alone in this fight for pure love. I know many holy women who have struggled with these temptations and addictions and have been restored by Christ. Now they are full of love, joy, and life again; and Christ desires to resurrect these same things in you. Read the quote below and make a choice about what type of love you will settle for in your life from this day forward—a mere shadow of all that love can be, or the real deal. The choice is yours, and Christ is waiting to remind you that you have been made to love, but also *to be loved in return.*

> A person's rightful due is to be treated as an object of love, not as an object for use. We are not the sum of our weaknesses and failures; we are the sum of the Father's love for us.—Pope St. John Paul II

5. No, the Church Is Not "Homophobic"

Why does the Catholic Church hate homosexuals? Do they think it is a sin to be born that way? Why the heck can't they get married? Don't they deserve happiness, too? Who are you to tell them who they can love?

I'm sure you've either heard or asked these questions on a regular basis. I know that we have. Homosexuality is another big topic in our world right now. It is a topic of confusion, hurt, misinformation, scientific studies, and even hatred by some. It is a very complex subject and emotions are always involved one way or another. Either we have a friend or family member who is homosexual and we feel defensive and hurt, or we have no connection to it in our personal lives and so are scared or judgmental of what we do not understand.

The Church's teachings, no matter what the topic, come down to two main points: how can we help get this person to heaven, and how can we help them find true love and joy here on Earth through Christ. They do this by trying to guide us to be as close as possible to all that we were created to be originally— as beings created for love.

The first thing to realize is that the Church loves *all* people. Period. No exceptions. Never, ever, will it say, "Oh, you did this sin, or you think this way . . . you can't be loved by God, and therefore by His Church." It's just not true! God loves all His children. He handcrafted each one and He wants to save each one, which means the Church does, too. If any member of any church has ever told you otherwise I am truly sorry; but please remember that this is human error, not God's error.

Unfortunately, when some people approach the subject of homosexuality with fear or uncertainty it can lead to negative results, such as high bullying rates. In a survey conducted in 2005, 82 percent of LGBT students experienced problems with bullying due to their sexual orientation, and some felt unsafe at, or didn't even come to school.[10] Just as a parent's heart is broken at the sight of her child's tears, our Father's heart breaks to see this. The *Catechism of the Catholic Church* itself says that those who experience homosexual desires "must be accepted with respect, compassion, and sensitivity. Every sign of unjust discrimination in their regard should be avoided. These persons are called to fulfill God's will in their lives and, if they are Christians, to unite to the sacrifice of the Lord's cross the difficulties they may encounter from their condition."[19] Every person is called to that same uniting in Christ and fulfilling of His purpose for us. All are called to community and love in His Church.

So if this is true, why does the Church teach what it teaches when it comes to homosexual marriage? It teaches this because homosexual desires are disordered from what sexual desires were originally made to be. Many factors can lead to a person's homosexuality: environmental, genetic, or very rarely, choice. No matter what the reason, though, it is a distancing from the original plan for those desires from the beginning of Creation. The plan for man and woman to become one is written not only into our psychological complementariness, but into the way our bodies fit together—the two halves completing one reproductive system. As we talked about in the section on contraception, when sex is used without the life-giving properties that it was created to have, it opens the possibility of lust and of using one another. The same goes here, because there are no life-giving abilities between two men or two women.

What does that mean for someone who has homosexual desires? That they are broken? We are all broken. This is merely another example of this and of the fall of our broken world. It reflects nothing about that person as an individual, just that his or her desires have been distorted, as all of ours are in different ways. None of us should hide from any piece of ourselves. If we do, we give it the power to burden our thoughts and hearts with negative self-doubts and fears. We give it the power to keep us from seeking community, from seeking those who can help us, counsel us, and walk with us. It can even keep us from turning to God.

Each person with homosexual desires is beautiful and loved. God wants them to be loved, but more than anything else He wants to love them and He wants to be with them one day in heaven, just as He does for all of us. That is why the Church does not support homosexual marriages. We have to remember that the purpose of our lives is not to get married. Instead, the purpose of our lives is to find the path, the vocation, that God has made for each of us and that will both fulfill us most while on Earth and lead us to heaven. For some that is marriage, yes. However, for those who truly have no attraction to the opposite gender, they should have no attraction to the idea of being one with someone of the opposite gender in marriage—the bringing together of man and woman. One of the main purposes of marriage, in addition to this oneness, is the creation of a family. This aspect helps to preserve love in its selfless and giving nature. Neither the oneness nor the procreative aspects of marriage are possible in homosexual unions, and this can lead to self-seeking desires and to using one another, leaving neither one fully fulfilled. Instead, those with homosexual desires are called to a different path—the path of chaste love and friendship that all unmarried people are called to as they find their specific place in this world.

What do we do with all of this? What does it mean for our lives? It means that we should love every single person we meet, regardless of whether they have homosexual or heterosexual desires, and seek to show them how much they truly matter. If you experience homosexual desires, then we want you to realize just how much you matter, how much you are loved, and that you should not fear that part of you. Instead, seek community and support in your journey to finding God's unique and beautiful plan for your life. You are not forgotten; you are loved and you are His.

6. The Avoided "A" Word

There are a million arguments we can make on every side of the abortion debate. It's a hot, taboo topic that everyone knows about and hates to bring up. We aren't here to talk politics, we're here to present some facts that maybe you've never heard before. No matter what faith, political party, or background you come from, abortion is a big topic in your world right now and worth knowing the truth about. We are talking about the actual scientific facts, about what life is, when it begins, the progression of life in the womb, and what abortion really is and does. We'll try to keep it short.

This is not a "pro-life versus pro-choice" fight; this is about a *woman*, and this is about a *baby*. All that we ask, as we've asked you many times before, is that you read this section with an open mind, ask theses questions for yourself, do the research for yourself, and don't settle for indifference.

A. What Is Life?

By dictionary definition, life is "the existence of an individual human being or animal, and is the condition that distinguishes animals and plants from inorganic matter."[25] For our purposes, we will focus on human life and adapt this definition to be: "the existence of an individual human being."

B. When Does Life Begin?

Biologically speaking, when the female egg and male sperm unite a zygote is formed. This zygote has its own unique set of forty-six chromosomes, half mother and half father; and therefore a separate set from that of the mother's genome. This means that the zygote is now foreign to the mother's DNA and has the blueprints necessary for its new life as it begins to grow. One truth is known about this zygote, or fetus, or whatever scientific word you may hear this new cluster of developing cells called, and that is: it is *new*. Something new has started, something new has been created, and something new is developing.

The response of the woman's body is proof of this "newness." Our immune systems, in simple terms, are basically designed to recognize *nonself,* or foreign objects, and to destroy them in order to protect *self.* That's how it is able to recognize a virus, harmful bacteria, or even a splinter, which is pretty amazing. This ability of our bodies is precisely why pregnancy has always been somewhat of a mystery to the scientific community. Why is it that the mother's body does not attack the zygote/fetus/baby, the "foreign being," and kill it? The University of Oxford has been one of many places to research this paradox, in which the mother's immunity leaves the "antigenically foreign fetus" untouched. They concluded that it takes a "combination of immune adaptations" to ensure "the success of the pregnancy."[12] Meaning that the mother's immune system has to be actively suppressed in order for the new life to survive. This would not happen if the fetus were simply still a part of the mother.

Some are even looking into this alteration in the mother's body as a possible way of adapting similar proteins in order to improve patient's tolerance to organ transplants. If the zygote is being called "antigenic," or genetically different from the mother, and is recognized in the same way that foreign tissue would be by the mother (yet does not kick in her immune system), it is clear that immediately after fertilization this *new* zygote is foreign and separate from the mother.

Also, this foreign zygote is now on the pathway to becoming independent, right? Meaning that if all goes right, somewhere between that moment and nine months later the baby will be born and will be able to fully support itself. So then we return to the original question: "When does life begin?"

We encourage you to watch a video that you can find at http://liveaction.org/inhuman/what-is-human-video/. In the video people, including medical personnel, are asked for answers to this very question. A doctor says, "Well, in my heart and in my mind, you know, life begins when the mother thinks it begins, not when anybody else thinks it begins. For some women, it's before they conceive; for some women, it's never. Even after they deliver, it's still a problem, not a baby."[29] Even after a mother delivers her child it is still not a baby in this doctor's opinion. So how do we decide who gets to draw the line of life? How are you going to decide what your stance on this is? The further forward you move your line from contraception, the more you are going to have to say that you know what makes a person's life worth living. That sounds like an incredibly dangerous decision.

C. Progression of Life in the Womb

Most of us have taken a biology class in our lifetime, and may have even watched a video showing the detailed development of new life, but some facts often are not included in academic courses, perhaps because they are seen as extra or unnecessary information. Take some time to look through this chart for yourself and even look up the sources if you want. A lot about the identity of this new life can be seen in the details:

TIME	DEVELOPMENTS
Conception	Fertilization; full set of 46 human chromosomes present.
5 Weeks	Heartbeat begins; brain, spinal cord, and heart developing.
7.5 Weeks	Reflexive response begins to develop; fingers begin to form.
9 Weeks	Hands move; neck turns; hiccups begin.
11.5 Weeks	Baby can yawn.
12 Weeks	Fingerprints forming; fingernails and toenails growing.
13 Weeks	Lips and nose fully formed; capable of complex facial expressions.
14 Weeks	Taste buds present.
15 Weeks	Response to soft touch.
18 Weeks	Stress hormone released in response to being poked with a needle.
20 Weeks	Voice box moves in similar way to crying seen after birth.
22 Weeks	Response to sounds.
26 Weeks	Blink-startle response to sudden loud noises.
28 Weeks	Sense of smell functions; eyes produce tears.
29 Weeks	Pupils react to light.
37 Weeks	Firm hand grip.

(See Bibliography, sources 1, 21, and 24.)

Every day premature babies are born and able to survive at many different stages in this development. Thanks to advances in medicine, these little ones fighting to survive outside of the womb before the expected time are able to live. As early as twenty-one weeks into the pregnancy, babies can survive outside of the womb;[2] and yet late-term abortions generally occur around twenty-four weeks.[9] That means that babies being killed through late-term abortion could have survived on their own. Those killed in earlier abortions may not be able to do that yet, but they are still a new human life and, as this chart shows, from conception to birth they begin exhibiting more and more recognizable human characteristics.

D. What Exactly Is an Abortion?

More than one million abortions happen each year just in the United States.[8] If you have never watched a video of an abortion, or looked up exactly what is done to both the mother and the child, please do it. It's something you need to know, even though it is hard. Before you can take a position on this topic you need to see the raw, unfiltered, real-life version of an abortion, not the fluffed up, "it's simple and harmless" version the media presents. You can visit our website for links or simply Google or YouTube it.

In some videos, the baby can be seen moving away from the needle inserted into the womb to kill it. In others, mutilated pieces of recognizable body parts are all that is left on the medical table after the baby has been removed from the mother. It's not as easy as the clinics tell you it is, and it's not simple and harmless for the mother, either.

Mothers often don't even understand what they are getting themselves into because they want to believe the lie that it is an easy fix to their fears out of sheer desperation. Afterward, however, they are left scarred and in much more pain than they thought they would be in, both physically and psychologically. Later in life these same women may not be able to have children, or when they do have children often feel the trauma of holding the same human life in their arms that they allowed to be killed in their womb long ago. It is hard to even begin to imagine this kind of agony.

If you are reading this, and this is you, then you have fallen victim to the trap of abortion and we implore you to please seek help. You do not have to go through this alone, and God truly wants nothing more than to heal you completely and restore love and joy to your life. We all fall. What is important is that we do not doubt the hope of Christ's love for us and His ability to make all things, even the seemingly impossible ones, new again.

When a woman becomes pregnant, she does indeed have a choice. She can choose whether or not she is in a place in her life to responsibly raise a child. However, the choice that neither she nor any doctor can make is the choice to kill her child. How can she or any other human decide whether another human being deserves to live or die? There are countless organizations set up to help women who are pregnant and scared, and even to find adoptive families for their babies if they are unable to take care of them. They will walk any woman through every step of her pregnancy so that she is never alone. So if this is you, know that you are not alone, and that the child within you is a beautiful gift, already with a big life ahead of him or her, and a plan written into that uniquely designed little heart.

We've presented you with a lot of information here, and it is only a fraction of what is out there. Know the facts, look up the videos, and watch what abortion is actually doing in our society. This is not a fetus or embryo or clump of cells that we are talking about. It is a human life, a baby in need of its mother. Please don't be one of so many to blindly defend what they know little about. Learn about it. This isn't just about a choice; this is about the gift of life and the recognition that no human can give life on his or her own.

> From the very moment of conception, and then of birth, the new being is meant to express fully his humanity, to "find himself" as a person. This is true for absolutely everyone, including the chronically ill and the disabled. "To be human" is his fundamental vocation: "to be human" in accordance with the gift received, in accordance with that "talent" which is humanity itself, and only then in accordance with other talents. In this sense God wills every man "for his own sake." In God's plan, however, the vocation of the human person extends beyond the boundaries of time. It encounters the will of the Father revealed in the Incarnate Word: God's will is to lavish upon man a sharing in His own divine life. As Christ says: "I came that they may have life and have it abundantly" (John 10:10).—Pope St. John Paul II

Conclusion: Now What?

As we've seen throughout this book, our world is broken. It is constantly surrounding women with conflicting lies regarding their beauty and the love they deserve. However, if we stop to see beyond these lies and untwist what has been twisted, our Father is there, always calling us back to the greatness that we were originally made for. Now more than ever is the time to speak up for *truth, beauty, love, and life.* Even though reading a book won't solve everything for you, it does offer you a chance to stop, to look around, and to apply a new perspective to your life.

What matters most is what you do from here. Our challenge to you is: ask questions, seek truth, be brave enough to make changes, be honest with yourself and where you're at, find your joy, discover your true beauty, and know that you are loved.

Every day you must make the choice between being the woman God created you to be and being a woman of this world. We aren't here to say we have all the answers, we definitely don't, but we're here to remind you that *you are not alone.* We know this isn't easy and we are fighting these struggles with you every day. It is not about knowing everything, but about taking everything we know and searching for the truth our generation and our world seems to have lost.

Our truth lies in a God who loves us beyond comprehension. Christ died so that we could know our worth—for we are loved beyond measure. We are Daughters of the King; His little girls, His beautiful creations.

Together, we can remind the world of this and restore true femininity, *one crown at a time.*

Do not be conformed to this world, but be transformed by the renewal of your mind, that you may prove what is the will of God, what is good, acceptable, and perfect. —Romans 12:2

For more information, advice, tips, links, or to contact us, check out our **website**: www.restoreyourcrown.com or send us an **e-mail** at: ContactM&K@restoreyourcrown.com

BIBLIOGRAPHY

1. "Abortion Procedures: American Pregnancy Explores Abortion." American Pregnancy Association. N.p.. 25 Apr. 2012. Web. 06 Mar. 2015.

2. Bates, Claire. "A Medical Miracle: World's Most Premature Baby, Born at 21 Weeks and Five Days, Goes Home to Her Delighted Parents." *Daily Mail.* 25 Apr. 2011. Web. 08 Mar. 2015.

3. "Birth Control Pills—Types, Effectiveness, and Side Effects of Birth Control Pills." WebMD.N.d. Web. 08 Mar. 2015.

4. "Facts About Alcoholism & Addiction." *Alcohol Abuse Statistics.* Foundation for a Drug- Free World. n.d. Web. 18 Jan. 2015.

5. Gilkerson, Luke. "Covenant Eyes." Covenant Eyes.com. 19 Feb. 2013. Web. 05 Dec. 2014.

6. Green, John. *The Fault in Our Stars.* New York: Dutton Penguin, 2010.

7. Haller, Madeline. "11 Qualities of the Perfect Woman." *Men's Health.* 9 Dec. 2012. Web. 06 Dec. 2014.

8. "Induced Abortion in the United States." Guttmacher Institute, July 2014. Web. 17 Jan. 2015.

9. Jacobson, Jodi. "Late Abortions: Facts, Stories, and Ways to Help." *RH Reality Check.* N.p. 02 June 2009. Web. 04 Mar. 2015.

10. "LGBT Bullying Statistics." NoBullying.com, 31 May 2014. Web. 17 Jan. 2015.

11. "Marriage and Divorce." American Psychological Association. N.p.. 2015. Web. 06 Jan. 2015.

12. "Maternal and Fetal Immune Responses during Pregnancy." *Europe PubMed*(1993): *Europe PubMed Central.* Nuffield Department of Obstetrics and Gynecology, University of Oxford, 1993. Web. 15 Jan. 2015.

13. "Media, Body Image, and Eating Disorders." National Eating Disorders Association. N.p., n.d. Web. 05 Dec. 2014.

14. "Media Influence." Eating Disorders and the Media. Radar Programs, 2014. Web. 04 Dec. 2014.

15. Nanda, Tavish. "Science And Religion Quotes: What World's Greatest Scientists Say About God." HuffingtonPost.com. 11 Feb. 2012. Web. 11 Jan. 2015.

16. "National Survey of Family Growth." Centers for Disease Control and Prevention, 21 Aug. 2013. Web. 09 Jan. 2015.

17. "Natural Family Planning Method As Effective As Contraceptive Pill, New Research Finds." ScienceDaily. 21 Feb. 2007. Web. 18 Jan. 2015.

18. *New American Standard Bible*. La Habra, CA: Foundation Publications, for the Lockman Foundation, 1971.

19. "Part Three: Life in Christ." *Catechism of the Catholic Church*, 2nd ed. Part 3, Section 2, Chapter 2, Article 6. Saint Charles Borromeo Catholic Church Web Site. Web. 10 Jan. 2015.

20. Pope John Paul II. "Letter to Families." Vatican, 1994. Web. 09 Jan. 2015.

21. "Prenatal Summary." The Endowment for Human Development. N.d. Web. 07 Mar. 2015.

22. "Religion: Behind Every Door: God." *Time*. 03 Dec. 1951. Web. 11 Jan. 2015.

23. Stanton, Glenn. "Premarital Sex and Greater Risk of Divorce." Focus on the Family. N.p. Apr. 2011. Web. 09 Jan. 2015.

24. Swiss Virtual Campus. "10.1 Early Development and Implantation." *The Embryoblast*. Human Embryology: Embryogenesis. N.d. Web. 07 Mar. 2015.

25. The Free Dictionary. Farlex, Inc. 2015. Web. 11 Jan. 2015.

26. Thompson, Jeff. "Is Nonverbal Communication a Numbers Game?" *Psychology Today.* N.p. 30 Sept. 2011. Web. 03 Mar. 2015.

27. Watson, Rita, MPH. "Oxytocin: The Love and Trust Hormone Can Be Deceptive." Psychology *Today.* 13 Oct. 2013. Web. 09 Jan. 2015.

28. West, Christopher. *Theology of the Body for Beginners.* West Chester, PA: Ascension, 2004.

29. "What Is Human?" *Inhuman: Undercover in America's Late-Term Abortion Industry.* N.p.. 13 June 2013. Web. 15 Jan. 2015.

30. "32 Shocking Divorce Statistics." McKinley Irvin Family Law. N.p. 30 Oct. 2012. Web. 09 Jan. 2015.